T0358259

Cambridge Elements ≡

Elements in the Economics of Emerging Markets
edited by
Bruno S. Sergi
Harvard University

MOBILE BANKING AND ACCESS TO PUBLIC SERVICES IN BANGLADESH

Influencing Issues and Factors

M. Kabir Hassan
University of New Orleans

Jannatul Ferdous
Comilla University

Hasanul Banna
Manchester Metropolitan University

CAMBRIDGE
UNIVERSITY PRESS

Shaftesbury Road, Cambridge CB2 8EA, United Kingdom

One Liberty Plaza, 20th Floor, New York, NY 10006, USA

477 Williamstown Road, Port Melbourne, VIC 3207, Australia

314–321, 3rd Floor, Plot 3, Splendor Forum, Jasola District Centre,
New Delhi – 110025, India

103 Penang Road, #05–06/07, Visioncrest Commercial, Singapore 238467

Cambridge University Press is part of Cambridge University Press & Assessment,
a department of the University of Cambridge.

We share the University's mission to contribute to society through the pursuit of
education, learning and research at the highest international levels of excellence.

www.cambridge.org
Information on this title: www.cambridge.org/9781009454025

DOI: 10.1017/9781009447089

When citing this work, please include a reference to the DOI 10.1017/9781009447089

First published 2024

A catalogue record for this publication is available from the British Library.

ISBN 978-1-009-45402-5 Hardback
ISBN 978-1-009-44709-6 Paperback
ISSN 2631-8598 (online)
ISSN 2631-858X (print)

Mobile Banking and Access to Public Services in Bangladesh

Influencing Issues and Factors

Elements in the Economics of Emerging Markets

DOI: 10.1017/9781009447089
First published online: February 2024

M. Kabir Hassan
University of New Orleans

Jannatul Ferdous
Comilla University

Hasanul Banna
Manchester Metropolitan University

Author for correspondence: M. Kabir Hassan, mhassan@uno.edu

Abstract: This Element examines the role of mobile banking in accessing public services in Bangladesh. It also identifies the key influencing factors and challenges in accessing public services through mobile banking and suggests policy measures to overcome these challenges. Based on a survey of 300 people, the study finds that mobile banking facilitates access to public services, which is beneficial and effective for both rural and urban users, as technology can increase the quality of work. Despite the benefits, some individuals are reluctant to use the service due to high transaction costs and a lack of digital literacy.

Keywords: mobile banking, public service, digital literacy, digital finance, Bangladesh

ISBNs: 9781009454025 (HB), 9781009447096 (PB), 9781009447089 (OC)
ISSNs: 2631-8598 (online), 2631-858X (print)

Contents

1 Introduction   1

2 Theoretical Framework and Literature Review   10

3 Present Scenario of Mobile Banking in Bangladesh   31

4 Mobile Banking in Access to Public Services and Key Influencing Factors   51

5 Summary, Recommendations, and Concluding Facts   62

Abbreviations   69

References   70

1 Introduction

1.1 Introduction

Finance plays a vital role in driving economic growth, particularly in asset-rich countries like Bangladesh. Access to financing is crucial for achieving inclusive financial growth and alleviating poverty. The development policy of the country recognizes that the lack of financial services expansion among impoverished and marginalized populations can impede socioeconomic progress. The benefits of an inclusive financial system are manifold for the economy (Bangladesh Bank, 2019). The global trend of internet and mobile technology has led to the widespread adoption of mobile business (m-commerce) worldwide (Rosa & Malter, 2003). While mobile banking usage is more popular and advanced in developing/emerging countries, there is limited research on consumers' perceptions and behavioral intentions toward its utilization (Himel et al., 2021). Banking has a rich history in this region, with initially only a few government-owned public banks offering financial services. In the early days, some banks based in Calcutta conducted business in this area. However, the banking industry has experienced substantial growth over time. The advent of computer technology, mobile phone technology, and the Internet has significantly transformed the industry's operations (Zubayer et al., 2019).

The integration of communication technology into the financial industry has revolutionized banking services in the twenty-first century. Modern technology-driven banking services, such as ATM service, online banking, and mobile banking, have empowered the banking sector to deliver fast and high-quality client service through multiple channels, including ATM service, mobile banking, and online banking. Among these services, mobile banking has emerged as a particularly suitable facility, enabling previously unbanked individuals to engage in financial transactions. Mobile banking involves conducting banking operations using a mobile device, typically a cell phone. It represents a collaborative effort between the banking sector and mobile operators, encompassing announcement services and electronic money to facilitate various banking tasks via mobile phones. The popularity of mobile banking is on the rise in emerging countries like Bangladesh, owing to the rapid advancements in technology and widespread usage of mobile phones (Jahan & Shahria, 2021).

The development of financial services in countries like Bangladesh is primarily driven by the competitive environment and the desire to capture a larger market share. This drive for innovation in finance has significantly contributed to economic development. Financial innovations have led to the expansion and dissemination of financial services, whether through the introduction of new products or the implementation of new methods.

Financial innovations bring benefits to both financial service providers, such as financial institutions, and service consumers, including depositors and borrowers. On the supply side, these benefits encompass the development of advanced financial products, enhanced efficiency, and reduced transaction costs. On the demand side, the technology acceptance model provides insights into factors influencing user adoption. According to this model, perceived usefulness and ease of use are the key determinants of user acceptance of technology. Lower transaction costs, improved security and convenience, and reduced transaction risk for clients contribute to this perception. In addition, technological innovation has a positive impact on output, efficiency, macroeconomic growth, and company performance (Akhter & Khalily, 2020).

Bangladesh's banking sector has a long history, dating back to the country's independence in 1971. Following independence, commercial operations in banking witnessed significant growth, necessitating the establishment of a robust banking system. The State Bank of Pakistan, which was under the control of the Pakistan government, was renamed Bangladesh Bank, or Central Bank of Bangladesh, in 1972. Presently, the country boasts nearly a hundred commercial and noncommercial banks. Fifty commercial banks cater to urban areas as well as several major rural regions. The citizens rely on these banks to save money, secure loans, and utilize other banking services to enhance their quality of life. With the continuous increase in GDP and per capita income, Bangladesh's banking sector has undergone substantial expansion over the years (Zubayer et al., 2019). Despite the creation of numerous bank branches and the participation of individuals in microfinance institutions (MFIs) and other economic organizations, a significant portion of the adult population in Bangladesh remains financially disadvantaged. Farmers, who play a crucial role in the economy, have limited access to bank financing. Additionally, economically vulnerable segments of the population include landless laborers, migrants, slum dwellers, minority groups, socially marginalized individuals, impoverished elderly individuals, and women. While urban areas also have financially disadvantaged groups, the majority of economically disadvantaged individuals reside in rural regions.

This Element aims to examine the current status of mobile banking in terms of accessing public services in Bangladesh. It focuses on identifying critical influencing factors and challenges associated with accessing public services through mobile banking. Furthermore, it proposes policy measures to overcome these challenges, thus promoting mobile banking and improving access to public services.

1.2 Objectives of the Study

Mobile financial services (MFSs) have gained tremendous popularity and become an essential method for conducting financial transactions, especially for individuals who lack access to traditional banking channels. Including these large populations within the MFS ecosystem holds significant socioeconomic importance, as mentioned in the previous section (Bangladesh Bank & University of Dhaka, 2017). The purpose of the study is to examine the following factors in Bangladesh:

1. To assess the present status of mobile banking in terms of accessing public services in Bangladesh.
2. To identify the key influencing factors and challenges associated with accessing public services through mobile banking.
3. To propose policy measures aimed at overcoming the challenges related to mobile banking and improving access to public services.

1.3 Statement of the Problem

E-banking provides customers with access to various information through computer, internet, and mobile phone platforms (Daniel, 1999). E-banking is the overarching term that encompasses all forms of electronic banking, including internet banking (I-banking) and mobile banking (m-banking). I-banking relies heavily on information communication and technology to achieve its objectives of 24-hour accessibility, minimal error rates, and swift transfer of financial services. While people often associate I-banking with bank websites, it encompasses more than just a well-designed site. Back-end systems such as account platforms, support applications like customer relationship management (CRM) platforms, communication tools like LINK to connect I-banking with payment systems, and middleware that integrate disparate systems are also essential. Consumers are attracted to these technologies due to their convenience, user-friendly interfaces in specific scenarios, cost-effectiveness, and potential cost savings. I-banking is seen as an advancement over traditional alternative delivery methods, allowing the financial system to expand its operations. However, m-banking emerges as a valuable technological solution provided by commercial banks, enabling clients to access a wide range of banking services in today's world. M-banking has revolutionized conventional notions of banking, in both low-income and high-income countries. It is considered an avenue to provide financial products to the unbanked poor, who are often overlooked by traditional financial institutions in low-income nations (Dona et al., 2014).

The development of financial products plays a significant role in the growth and economic progress of countries like Bangladesh, driven by competitiveness in monetary markets and the pursuit of increased market share. The competitiveness and expansion of financial services are greatly influenced by innovation and technological advancements, which contribute to improved efficiency and effectiveness at both the macroeconomic and firm-level institutional levels. The perceived utility and ease of use are critical factors influencing the acceptance of technology among users. Positive perceptions regarding the usefulness and user-friendliness of financial services are influenced by factors such as low transaction costs, enhanced security measures, improved convenience, and reduced transaction risk. Among the various advancements in the financial sector, mobile technology stands out as a multidimensional innovation with far-reaching effects. It promotes efficiency and fosters financial inclusion on a technological level (Akhter & Khalily, 2017).

Customers can conveniently perform a range of transactions using e-banking, including account transfers, balance inquiries, online loan or credit card applications, and bill payments, all without the need to visit a physical bank. M-banking offers round-the-clock services, cost-effective transactions, enhanced security measures, increased transaction volumes in shorter time-frames, and improved transaction accuracy compared to traditional banking methods (Nasri, 2011). During the COVID-19 crisis, a significant portion of the agent base in MFSs remains partially active due to movement restrictions and closures of physical marketplaces. MFS providers face two major challenges in ensuring liquidity for e-money and cash at agent points and facilitating cash settlements across banks during reduced banking hours. However, approved MFS providers like bKash in Bangladesh continue to process approximately 5.8 million daily transactions. Customers are utilizing bKash services for various purposes, including money transfers, bill payments, and merchant transactions for essential items like food and pharmaceuticals. In addition to cash transactions at agent locations, bKash customers can quickly transfer money from any bank account, Visa, or MasterCard to their bKash account. The Bangladeshi community working overseas also utilizes scheduled banks to directly transfer remittances to targeted beneficiaries' bKash accounts. As a result, bKash effectively meets people's transactional needs during the ongoing crisis (Dalim, 2020).

Mobile banking services not only provide essential information but also offer notifications through SMS. In Bangladesh, the affordability of mobile prices, which are currently at the second-lowest level in history, makes mobile banking and other cellphone services crucial. By expanding its mobile banking services, Bangladesh has the potential to position itself ahead in terms of e-governance

(Rahman, 2016). M-banking services are rapidly gaining popularity in Bangladesh as people's willingness to embrace new technologies grows. This presents significant opportunities for the country's existing banks and financial institutions. Bangladesh Bank actively encourages banks and financial organizations to develop m-banking services, with private commercial banks, both locally and internationally, offering more advanced m-banking services compared to state-owned commercial banks (Huda & Chowdhury, 2017). Banks are striving to offer new and improved m-banking services to attract and retain customers. However, despite increasing demand from both general consumers and the business community, m-banking is still in its early stages of development. Several factors contribute to this, including a lack of secure and reliable information infrastructure, inadequate internet connectivity, high internet charges, limited IT literacy among customers, a lack of legal and supervisory frameworks, and high investment requirements for adopting new technologies (Sadekin & Shaikh, 2016).

The use of e-services has become increasingly prevalent in Bangladesh, encompassing a wide range of activities such as publishing admission test results, job applications for overseas positions, registration for pilgrimages, delivery of official documents, online submission of digital tenders, tax returns, mobile banking, and more (Rahman, 2016). Examples of additional e-services include SMS-based complaint submission to police stations, online utility bill payments, efficient communication with individuals working abroad, and the introduction of e-passports. To enhance m-banking services nationwide, Bangladesh Bank must undertake several innovative measures. Commercial banks also need to embrace new technologies to integrate them into their banking operations, ensuring customer satisfaction and effectively addressing global challenges. While this concept is relatively new in Bangladesh, it holds significant potential. The findings of this study will provide valuable insights to other researchers and policymakers regarding the intricacies and possibilities of mobile banking. The current study aims to analyze the current state of mobile banking in relation to public service access in Bangladesh. It will identify key factors influencing mobile banking adoption and explore the barriers that hinder public benefit from these services. Finally, the study will propose policy changes to address the challenges faced by mobile banking and improve access to public services.

1.4 Rationale of the Study

International leaders have recognized the crucial role of information and communication technologies (ICTs) in achieving global development goals.

The aim is to leverage modern technologies to foster the development of twenty-first-century skills across various fields, including science, mathematics, and English language, by utilizing cost-effective delivery mechanisms and digital learning content. This approach seeks to enhance productivity and align with the demands of the globalized world in the twenty-first century (GoB, 2010). The potential of ICTs to drive progress is reflected in the Sustainable Development Goal (SDG) on universal internet access. As digital technologies become pervasive across all sectors of the economy and society, ICTs and ICT-based activities are expected to have an impact on all 17 SDGs (Hernandez, 2019). This component aims to establish sustainable connectivity solutions that extend the benefits of Digital Bangladesh to the most marginalized and disadvantaged communities. Key focus areas include the development of inclusive access points, community awareness and capacity building for public e-services, production of local language and culturally relevant content, and the establishment of interactive platforms to enhance grassroots engagement in policy discussions (GoB, 2010).

Technological advancements have enabled banks to enhance the performance of their distribution channels, with electronic banking referring to innovations in the banking sector that leverage electronic delivery methods. Electronic commerce, including ATMs, mobile banking, PC banking, telebanking, and online banking, has brought about a revolutionary shift in the financial industry. These innovations aim to provide a payment system that can keep pace with the demands of the digital marketplace. Notably, the idea of conducting transactions via mobile phones, even without the need for internet connectivity at the user level, has gained momentum due to the widespread availability of cellular connections (Hossain & Haque, 2014).

Most bank branches are situated in state, district, and upazila (Kumar, 2022). Financial service providers have recently introduced mobile banking as their latest financial technology, allowing customers to access their accounts, obtain information, transfer funds between accounts, and make payments via the Internet. This enables customers to bank anytime and anywhere in the country, providing them with a comprehensive range of services (Baua & Akber, 2021).

There has been a lack of comprehensive research on digital literacy that specifically focuses on populations with limited access and exposure to information and communication technologies, such as rural families in Bangladesh. Additionally, prior to this study, no surveys had been conducted in Bangladesh to gather detailed and systematic data on key factors, including domestic-level digital literacy, domestic socioeconomic status and systems, household-level usage and engagement with various public e-services, and the challenges faced in accessing public e-services. Consequently, the existing digital literacy frameworks are inadequate for contexts with limited access and exposure. The digital literacy measurement developed in this study is expected to be unique and fill the gap in the literature, providing detailed insights into digital skills that will inform and contribute to future advancements in digital service usage (Shadat et al., 2020).

Despite its appealing features, m-banking adoption in Bangladesh encounters several challenges. This study focuses on the customer's perspective regarding the uptake of mobile banking in Bangladesh. The study aims to answer the following questions:

(a) What is the present status of mobile banking in access to public services in Bangladesh?
(b) What are the key influencing factors and challenges in access to public services through mobile banking?

By addressing these questions, the study aims to shed light on the status and challenges of mobile banking adoption in accessing public services in Bangladesh.

1.5 Methodology of the Study

The objective of the study was to investigate the challenges and potential of mobile banking in Bangladesh. To obtain the required data, a survey was conducted among diverse age groups, and the collected data was analyzed in relation to the study's objectives. The study heavily relied on field data collection to gather essential information (Ahmed et al., 2012).

The methodology employed in this study encompasses a set of general principles or guidelines that serve as the foundation for developing specific techniques or approaches to understand and address various issues within a specific field. It is important to emphasize that methodology is a collection of practices rather than a rigid formula.

1.5.1 Sampling Procedure and Collection of Data

The research data was validated through the collection of both primary and secondary sources. Primary data was directly obtained from firsthand sources using methods such as questionnaire surveys, observation, and experimentation. The information gathered from the respondents was unpublished and unprocessed. The data collection process involved distributing organized questionnaires to participants capable of completing them. A random sample of 500 people was chosen, and a total of 300 completed surveys were returned, resulting in an 85 percent favorable response rate. Secondary data, on the other hand, was gathered from various sources such as books, journals, magazine articles, and newspaper stories.

1.5.2 Research Instrument Development and Pretesting

A questionnaire was developed by considering the norms of previous studies as the central ideas (Bisschoff & Clapton, 2014). The development process involved refining ideas and phrasing to align with the context of the financial sector in Bangladesh. The questionnaire comprised multiple sections that addressed the features provided by mobile banking services. These sections focused on accessibility, users' attitudes toward the services, perceived service marketing, and promotional activities. These areas were considered crucial in assessing customer satisfaction and the overall service quality of the banks. The questionnaire consisted of seventeen questions organized into four subsections that evaluated the aforementioned aspects. The tool utilized a five-point scale for data collection. Additionally, the questionnaire included a section where respondents could provide demographic details. Initially, a prototype structured questionnaire was created for pretesting, and necessary modifications were made before finalizing the instrument.

1.5.3 Data Analysis

The researcher conducted a structured questionnaire survey. The questionnaires were distributed to 500 randomly selected respondents, and 300 completed questionnaires were collected, checked, and coded. The researcher conducted various descriptive analyses through charts and tables using the collected data. Data input accuracy was cross-checked by the researcher to ensure reliability. Subsequently, the data were entered into the SPSS (Statistical Package for Social Sciences) software for further analysis. All statistical analyses were conducted using the SPSS software.

1.6 Conclusion

Mobile banking has gained significant prominence in Bangladesh's financial system and is expected to continue its growth trajectory. The primary objective of this study is to evaluate the potential of mobile banking in Bangladesh. Mobile banking encompasses financial services provided by commercial banks in collaboration with mobile telecom operators, leveraging technological advancements. The expansion of mobile financial services relies on advancements in technology and the trust placed by consumers in the offered services. Bangladesh has made remarkable strides toward financial inclusion by providing adequate financial support to the underprivileged through alternative delivery methods like digital money (Khatun et al., 2021). The convergence of internet and mobile networks creates new possibilities and opportunities. Viewing mobile banking as a mere extension of traditional web-based services might overlook unique differentiating characteristics and potential value-added opportunities. Mobile banking is recognized as one of the most important and valuable mobile services available, revolutionizing the service framework and offering a customer-centric approach to studying its value proposition. This study further examines key factors influencing the adoption of mobile banking, identifies barriers, and explores future prospects for success (Ayadi, 2005). With the advancements in mobile technologies and devices, banking users can conveniently perform financial transactions from anywhere and at any time. Several global banks have already enabled access to financial data through smartphones. Consequently, it is essential to investigate the factors influencing users' inclination toward mobile banking (Ahmed et al., 2012).

Through internet banking, users can conveniently conduct financial transactions. However, this convenience is dependent on internet connectivity, and users may face limitations when they are not connected to the Internet, such as when they are on a bus or having a meal at a restaurant. Mobile banking, on the other hand, offers 24/7 convenience as users have continuous access to their mobile phones throughout the day. To achieve a truly convenient banking experience, it is important to explore mobile banking options, hence the need for m-banking (Andrew, 2009). Mobile banking enables customers to perform various financial transactions from the comfort of their homes or nearby agent locations, such as bill payments (gas, electricity, water), mobile recharges, money transfers, adding funds, and credit card bill payments. However, it is worth noting that these services have increased the commercial overhead costs for mobile financial service providers (Dalim, 2020). Mobile financial services have simple requirements for access. Users need a National Identification Card (NID) to create an account and utilize the services. In rural areas, where literacy levels and economic development are lower compared to urban areas, it can be challenging to establish local banks and provide banking services. However, mobile financial services can be easily accessed and utilized with just a mobile phone, an agent, and a small amount of money. This Element examines the challenges and potential of mobile financial services in Bangladesh and provides recommendations on how this service can be a great alternative to traditional banking (Kumar, 2022). The next section of this Element focuses on the theoretical framework and literature review.

2 Theoretical Framework and Literature Review

2.1 Introduction

Globally, digitization is transforming various aspects of people's lives, including education, lifestyle, work, and communication. The digitalization of public and private services aims to enhance accessibility for users, and as a result, digital literacy is increasingly crucial in maximizing the benefits of these services. Without essential digital skills, the advantages of ICT-driven public programs may not reach all citizens of a country. Bangladesh, aspiring to become a fully digitalized nation, faces similar challenges in this regard (Shadat et al., 2020). Technology no longer holds a dominant position solely in specific industries; it has become integral for organizations to keep up with the ever-evolving business world. The banking industry, like many others, is no exception. Technological advancements have already had a significant impact on the functioning of banks and will continue to do so in the future. This study focuses on mobile financial systems to understand their operations and analyze their usage, thus shedding light on their role in Bangladesh (Ehsan, 2019).

The mobile phone, an ICT innovation, has demonstrated promising potential for economic opportunities and social development (Rashid & Elder, 2009). It is widely acknowledged that disparities in internet access contribute to socioeconomic inequality (van Deursen et al., 2019). Over the past few decades, the digital divide has grown rapidly, and scholars have examined various factors to explain these disparities (Blank & Groselj, 2014; Ono & Zavodny, 2007; Zillien & Hargittai, 2009). The concept of "e-inclusion" has emerged as a contentious topic due to the widening digital gap. The digital divide is a complex issue influenced by multiple political, social, educational, economic, and geographical factors, including income, race, gender, awareness, age, geographic location, culture, attitudes, and skills (Carr, 2007). Cross-country data shows that poverty and education are significant predictors of digital disparities at the primary and secondary levels (Hilbert, 2010). Age also plays a role in determining the digital divide, with younger age groups, typically those aged 12–59, being more likely to utilize the Internet than older individuals (Madden & Fox, 2006).

The digital divide encompasses two levels: the first-level digital gap, which pertains to differences in individuals' access to internet infrastructure, and the second-level digital divide, which refers to disparities in individuals' online skills and internet usage (Newhagen & Bucy, 2005; Zillien & Hargittai, 2009). While internet accessibility is a fundamental requirement for digital inclusion, the focus of the digital divide discussion has shifted in recent years toward the development of online skills (i.e., the second-level digital gap). These skills are essential for effectively and efficiently utilizing the Internet. Therefore, the digital divide encompasses both disparities in internet access and online abilities, recognizing that internet access has positive implications while online skills play a critical role (Siddiquee & Islam, 2020). Mobile phones have become a vital tool worldwide, providing individuals with access to information on various aspects such as healthcare, education, weather, news, job opportunities, financial services, and stock market updates. The increased use of mobile phones in developing countries has contributed to the improvement of monetary systems, government services, citizen feedback mechanisms, and other beneficial outcomes (Canuto, 2013).

In recent decades, governments worldwide have embraced e-governance, a process that utilizes ICT to make government services accessible to the public. By implementing e-governance, governments can achieve development objectives, enhance service quality, improve service delivery processes, and ensure efficiency, transparency, accountability, and responsiveness in the public sector. Furthermore, it provides citizens with opportunities to engage in democratic institutions and processes (Mahajan, 2015). The benefits of mobile phones, on the other hand, have been particularly significant in rural areas (Sarma & Pais, 2011), where marginalized and financially underserved populations reside. Despite possessing mobile phones, these individuals face financial disadvantages. In Bangladesh, limited access to finance is recognized as a significant obstacle in the fight against poverty. During the pandemic, government regulations governing various mobile banking activities have increased people's electronic financial access, particularly for peer-to-peer cash transactions, wage payments, utility bill settlements, and more. As a result, people's behavior has shifted toward digital transactions, making it easier for them to access money. To foster a cashless society, the government should integrate seamless access to financial services platforms within the country (Khatun et al., 2021).

Bangladesh experiences a substantial digital divide between rural and urban areas, primarily driven by economic and wealth disparities. The imbalance in ICT adoption between rural and urban regions further exacerbates the disparities in economic and social growth (Brixiova, 2009). The Government of Bangladesh (GoB) recognizes the need to bridge the socioeconomic development gap between rural and urban areas and is actively working to address the digital divide at both the first and second levels. Closing this gap is a pressing concern and a significant challenge for policymakers, practitioners, and academics in the country (Billon et al., 2009). This section encompasses the conceptual framework, literature review, and analytical framework, laying the foundation for the subsequent discussions.

2.2 Conceptual Framework

2.2.1 Mobile Banking

The term "mobile banking" refers to the provision and utilization of banking services through mobile phones. The increased adoption of ICT within the financial and banking industry has paved the way for a new, innovative, and cost-effective channel for delivering financial and banking services. Mobile banking utilizes the same technology as e-banking (Welch, 1999), enabling banks to conduct swift wireless or internet-based business operations (Greenacre & Buckley, 2014). Transactions performed through mobile devices such as mobile phones and personal digital assistants (PDAs) are categorized as mobile banking (Georgi & Pinkl, 2005). Mobile banking, also known as m-banking, SMS banking, and other similar terms, allows individuals to carry out financial transactions such as checking account balances, transferring funds, and paying bills using a mobile phone or PDA connected to the Internet. This can be accomplished through various means, including the phone's web browser, dedicated software provided by the bank, or through short messaging service (SMS). Customers who have a mobile phone and have enrolled in mobile banking services can utilize these methods to conduct their banking transactions. Mobile banking has provided benefits to both customers and banks, saving them time and money. The initial mobile banking services were offered through text messages, and with the introduction of rudimentary smartphones equipped with WAP technology, allowing mobile web access, European banks began offering mobile banking to their clients in 1999. Mobile banking encompasses the delivery and utilization of banking and financial services through mobile communication devices (Parvin, 2013).

E-money, sometimes referred to as "mobile banking," is a method of storing value that meets certain criteria: (i) it is issued with a receipt; (ii) it consists of digitally recorded data stored on a device such as a server, card, or mobile phone; (iii) it can be used as a form of payment by parties other than the issuer; and (iv) it can be converted back into cash. Convertibility distinguishes e-money from other nonconvertible payment instruments like credit cards, store gift vouchers, and airtime. E-money issuers can include payment gateways, credit issuers, or telecommunications companies. In this Element, we focus on "nonbank" e-money issuers, also known as "providers." In many e-money systems, cash and e-money are typically exchanged at the provider's agents, which can include retail businesses such as shops and gas stations. Mobile phones are commonly used for payments between e-money consumers (Greenacre & Buckley, 2014). The primary advantage of mobile banking is that it enables banks to serve their customers even without internet access or extensive technological knowledge. This eliminates the need for customers to be physically present beside computers to access the services mentioned (Ahmed et al., 2012).

Many countries have implemented mobile banking as a means to reach rural populations for financial inclusion and leverage the mobility and technology independence it offers (Banna et al., 2021). The concept behind including unbanked individuals in the financial system is to facilitate access to economic benefits such as improved savings, credit availability, income generation, and protection against economic instability (Donner & Tellez, 2008). Mobile banking provides various services such as mini-statements and account history checking, account activity alerts based on predefined thresholds, monitoring of term deposits, direct access to loan statements, connection to card reports, account statements, insurance plan administration, and pension scheme administration. It also enables actions like stopping payment on a check, ordering check books, checking account balances, reviewing transaction details, and making timely payments (Payne et al., 2008). Despite its significant potential, only a few banks in Bangladesh have adopted mobile banking thus far (Baten & Kamil, 2010). The government stands to benefit from capital investments from previously untapped sources, increased transaction transparency, enhanced tax potential, and improved circulation of funds that are currently not in the formal banking system.

2.2.2 Inception of Mobile Banking and Its Progress

As financial institutions redefine the role of banks, mobile banking has emerged as a valuable offering in the market. Banks have traditionally handled a significant portion of monetary transactions and safeguarded people's funds. Over time, banking systems have continuously evolved, with information technology playing a crucial role in establishing flexible payment methods and consumer banking sectors (Dixit & Datta, 2010a). Mobile banking represents one of the most modern services offered by banks, empowering individuals with significant financial capabilities. Through their mobile devices, people can now access their account balance, transaction history, bank products, and transfer funds anytime and from anywhere. Furthermore, mobile banking contributes to reducing fraud in the banking industry. The emergence of new economic associations often arises from unmet needs, inspiring innovative ideas and breakthroughs. These developments necessitate institutional adoptions, including the convergence between the banking industry and the telecommunications sector, giving rise to the concept of Mobile Banking (Ashta, 2017). Mobile banking is a fundamental aspect of the modern banking paradigm, aiming to digitize banking services. It has the potential to expand financial access to low-income individuals who are currently underserved by traditional bank branches. By reducing delivery costs, such as the expenses associated with establishing and maintaining physical distribution channels, mobile banking offers cost-saving benefits to both banks and customers (Ivatuary & Mas, 2010).

Nowadays, the banking sector is undergoing revolutionary transformations (Anyasi & Otubu, 2009). However, a substantial portion of the population remains outside the traditional banking industry. To attract and serve these individuals, mobile banking has proven to be highly effective. It has emerged as a catalyst for economic stability and technology-driven solutions that combat corruption and foster economic growth (Banna et al., 2021). Banking is a delicate business as it involves handling money and providing services. Establishing a strong relationship between the bank and its clients is therefore crucial. Mobile banking plays a vital role in enhancing consumer satisfaction as banking is a two-way street. It ensures that the bank operates in a cost-effective manner while meeting the needs of the customers. Mobile banking offers a wide range of services that surpass traditional methods. With a mobile phone, money transfers can be initiated at any time (Parvin, 2013). Mobile banking enables customers to conduct banking transactions irrespective of time, location, or internet access (Chitungo & Munongo, 2013). It has opened doors for millions of geographically isolated and unbanked individuals to participate in economic progress. However, in Bangladesh, the mobile banking market has remained relatively small compared to overall banking activities. The widespread use of cell phones does not automatically translate into widespread acceptance of mobile banking (Yu, 2012). Countries like Guatemala, Iran, and Mexico have embraced mobile banking, providing access to banking services through mobile phones. Pakistan has also made strides in mobile banking, although its scope is limited compared to India's more extensive offerings. Brazil, China, and Kenya have experienced significant growth in mobile banking user numbers, with an increase of over 100 percent. Furthermore, banks in countries such as the United Kingdom, the United States, South Korea, Singapore, and Sweden are now offering innovative mobile banking services to their customers (Khraim et al., 2011).

MFS facilitates quick, cost-effective, and simple transactions. In addition to basic transactions, users can access savings, credit, and insurance services. Through options such as m-wallets and micro-loans, including micro health or crop-failure insurance, these services help the unbanked population gain access to financial services (BCG, 2011). Technological advancements and institutional diversification have transformed the landscape of economic literacy and investment institutions. This shift has moved from traditional post office and bank branch banking to branchless banking. This development carries several implications, including: (a) suitability and payment properties: mobile devices enable households and firms to conveniently pay for utilities, (b) economic inclusion impact: mobile devices lead to a higher provision of financial services and enhance financial security, promoting economic inclusion, (c) organizational effect: institutions now have the ability to extend financial services to previously unreachable regions, supporting both firms and households, and (d) business confidence effect: new institutions can now offer access to finance for previously excluded firms and households in inaccessible areas. The list of potential implications of MFS can be significantly longer when addressing all financial actions at the micro-level (Akhter & Khalily, 2020).

In Bangladesh, there are currently twenty-eight licensed banks providing mobile banking services. As of December 2018, eighteen banks have already implemented mobile banking, with DBBL and BRAC Bank being the two leading players in the market (Akhter & Khalily, 2020). Mobile banking is widely used by both impoverished and well-off individuals due to its convenience (Akhter & Khalily, 2020). The primary reasons people use mobile banking in Bangladesh are for money transfers and security purposes. According to Bangladesh Bank (2012), over three-quarters of users utilize mobile banking for money transfers, and one-quarter use it for security-related transactions. Digital access refers to individuals or groups' access and ownership of various digital electronic devices and networks. Among these technologies, mobile phones, PCs, and the Internet are the most prominent access points for digital access (Shadat et al., 2020).

In metropolitan areas, mobile banking is primarily used for payment systems, while distant users rely on mobile banking to receive sent funds. The future growth of mobile banking is expected as nearly three-quarters of customers express their interest in using it. With a more widespread mobile network and appropriate regulations, MFS will contribute significantly to overall financial inclusion (Akhter & Khalily, 2020). The regulatory framework in Bangladesh allows the bank-led model to operate, setting criteria for MFS provision through Bangladeshi banks. Permissible MFS include disbursement from inward remittances, cash in/out through agents/ATMs/bank branches/mobile operator's outlets, business-to-person (B2P) payments, person-to-business (P2B) outflows, person-to-government (P2G) payments, and government-to-person (G2P) payments (Akhter & Khalily, 2020). In Bangladesh, digital behavior among customers is not as well established as in neighboring, western, or Southeast Asian environments. MFS providers such as bKash, Nagad, Rocket, Tcash, and Ukash have enrolled 102.80 million Bangladeshi consumers, but only 34.64 million are active clients. While digital payments account for around 1 percent of daily transactions in developing nations, the ratio is over 60 percent in wealthy countries.

Since the 1980s, financial institutions have aimed to meet clients' needs more efficiently. ATMs and internet banking were significant advancements, but they faced limitations in terms of portability and internet connectivity. In contrast, mobile phones are portable and widely used. Mobile phones with text messaging and web capabilities provide a great medium for banks to offer a wide range of services, making mobile banking a crucial factor in the industry (bankinfobd.com). In an era of globalization and digitization, mobile banking has emerged as a transformative force in the banking industry. It enables money management without the need for physical currency, which is vital for organizations. Correct and intelligent management of mobile banking presents tremendous opportunities for banks to maximize wealth and bring the unbanked into the financial system (Parvin, 2013). However, Bangladesh lags behind its major South Asian counterparts in terms of mobile banking adoption (Himel et al., 2021). Several barriers have hindered consumer adoption of MFS in the country, including issues of theft, security concerns, and a lack of trust in the system among agents, customers, and distributors (Yesmin et al., 2019).

2.2.3 Advantages of Mobile Banking

The mobile platform offers a convenient and alternative way to manage money without the need for physical currency. Mobile banking is seen as a potential option by mobile phone companies, while banks and financial organizations view it as a means to serve the unbanked population. Government authorities recognize its attractiveness but also address taxation and security concerns. Interestingly, there is a lack of academic studies on the impact of mobile banking systems on emerging economies (Bangladesh Bank & University of Dhaka, 2017). Mobile phone banking has the potential to provide low-cost virtual bank accounts to a significant portion of the unbanked population worldwide. Decreasing prices of airtime, competition, and the ability of electronic banking solutions to offer a wide range of services at low costs are driving this change (Ahmed et al., 2012). In Bangladesh, the expanding mobile network has led to increased mobile usage, smartphone usage, and internet services. Technological advancements have facilitated the development of smartphone banking services. The use of technology in metropolitan areas influences consumer behavior, payment methods, and shopping patterns. Mobile banking is widely used by people at all levels as a simple, cost-effective, secure, and convenient method for sending and receiving money. It also plays a significant role in providing financial services such as bill payments, cash deposits, fund transfers, and withdrawals via mobile telecommunications, contributing to improved efficiency and financial inclusion (Bangladesh Bank & University of Dhaka, 2017).

MFS have a significant impact on family households and small and medium-sized businesses in Bangladesh. Mobile money transfers are particularly popular among households, providing assistance during financial emergencies, loans, and loss or theft of funds. MFS also contributes to improved food intake, timely delivery of medications, and access to healthcare services. It supports family farming by ensuring a steady supply of seeds, labor, and water (Bangladesh Bank & University of Dhaka, 2017). Traditional banks with physical branches require customers to visit in person for essential banking tasks, while digital banks have minimal physical presence, performing core services digitally. Mobile banking has resulted in significant changes in financial products and institutional structures (Akhter & Khalily, 2020). Mobile banking provides customers and agents with a convenient, reliable, user-friendly, and secure transaction mechanism, allowing for account management, fund transfers, transaction status viewing, PIN and password changes, account locking, minimum balance alerts, check book requests, insurance policy management, bill payment alerts, and location-based services. It offers on-demand banking, acts as a mobile wallet, is convenient, fast, simple, and secure, solving the challenges of online banking (Parvin, 2013).

According to BCC (2011), mobile financial institutions have identified five key advantages over traditional banks when it comes to providing financial services to unbanked and underbanked individuals in Bangladesh. One of the advantages is the ability for customers to access their accounts 24/7 and conduct various transactions with ease. Additionally, digital banks can carry out transactions at a faster rate compared to traditional banks due to the absence of a paper-based approval system. The automation of digital banking services further contributes to their efficiency. With fewer physical branches and staff, digital banks have significantly lower expenses compared to traditional banks, enabling them to offer services at a lower cost to end users. In contrast, traditional banks rely on manual paper processing, which is prone to human errors. In digital banks, all data and information processing is automated, resulting in a higher level of accuracy. Furthermore, digital banks have the potential to provide access to finance for many new clients by leveraging a comprehensive database of consumer transaction profiles to construct credit profiles and offer loans based on these profiles. Digital banks are also known for their adaptability to new technologies and their ability to quickly introduce new services to clients. Many digital banks have successfully provided consumers with additional services, such as frequent expenditure reports, spending estimates, and collaborations with other financial applications (Hossain, 2021).

In terms of the banking experience of Bangladeshi consumers, new digital banking services encounter both advantages and obstacles. Initially, there may be challenges in understanding the use of digital banking, especially for individuals who are unbanked. Some banks in other countries offer online demos, but in many cases, physical demonstrations may be necessary to educate Bangladeshis about the use of digital banking. Since digital banks operate solely online, they become logical targets for unethical hackers, particularly those involved in ransomware attacks. Digital banks are inherently more vulnerable to cyberattacks and associated risks. All transactions with a digital bank are conducted online, which means that if a user's digital identification is stolen or compromised, their entire account balance is at risk. Additionally, all digital bank transactions rely on internet connectivity. Therefore, there is a significant reliance on a constant and reliable internet connection, and if the internet connection fails, the digital bank account becomes inaccessible (Hossain, 2021).

An Emphasis on "Long-Tail" Clients
Telcos have a lot of expertise in identifying and understanding their customers' demands, which allows them to deepen and widen their existing client connections. On the other hand, banks have traditionally focused their efforts on the wealthiest customers, ignoring the "long tail," which they will be unable to serve financially.

Customers Have Control over Critical Infrastructure
Mobile phone users already have the capacity to access MFS because their phone SIM card can function as a secure identification and authentication device.

Relationships with Customers
Many unbanked have already contacts with mobile operators, allowing them to access their usage history. Telcos gain an advantage in knowing who their potential financial services clients are and where they live due to this. It provides them with data on transaction patterns, which may be used to develop a credit history and a reliable means of communicating with customers.

Recognized Brand
The general public has had few contacts with major, formal financial institutions, resulting in a "trust gap" that may operate as a barrier to financial

inclusion. Telecom businesses, on the other hand, are often well known even among the lowest members of society, are regarded as safe, and are connected with instant communication – for example, through texting or SMS.

Extensive Distribution Network
Unlike traditional banks, telcos have a statewide network of traders who act as commissioned agents behind them. These businesses have a lot of experience dealing with these partners on price and product distribution.

2.3 Literature Review

With the widespread use of smartphones, mobile banking has experienced significant growth and popularity. As a result, it has become an essential area of study for bankers who aim to incorporate new features into mobile banking while maintaining existing value-added services (Jahan & Shahria, 2021). However, mobile banking is not widely adopted among Bangladeshi families. Its utility is currently limited mainly to money transfers and modest savings. Bangladeshi families have raised multiple concerns regarding mobile financial services, including poor network connectivity, incompatible phones, and expensive fees associated with MFS. Resolving these issues would contribute to the increased popularity of these services among Bangladeshi households.

On the other hand, small and medium-sized enterprises (SMEs) in Bangladesh are increasingly embracing MFS. The study results indicate that a majority of SMEs utilize MFS to expand their customer base and increase sales revenue. The most common transactions conducted by these organizations using MFS are revenue collection and supplier payments. Small and medium-sized businesses employ mobile banking to transfer payments between accounts or check their account balance at the end of the day. According to the respondents, MFSs have a positive impact on the revenue and profitability of the surveyed companies. However, it should be noted that MFS adoption does not directly correlate with efforts to reduce costs or increase investment. Nevertheless, most of the surveyed businesses agree that they will increase their usage of MFS transactions in the future (Bangladesh Bank & University of Dhaka, 2017).

Mobile banking in Bangladesh still has a long way to go. To ensure customer satisfaction with mobile banking, it is crucial for the banking sector, mobile carriers, regulatory bodies, and all other relevant parties to move forward with a constructive strategy. One unique aspect of this study's findings is the distinct perspective it reveals from younger customers. While previous studies on mobile banking in Bangladesh have identified trust, security, and assurance as the dominant factors in defining consumer satisfaction, this study reveals that cost is the most influential component, with security and convenience having less impact (Islam et al., 2019; Kabir, 2013). Realizing the benefits of digital banks also relies on effective administration. Traditional banks have historically been owned and operated by families or small groups. Consequently, key managerial positions are often filled by family members or close associates who may not possess the necessary skill set to efficiently operate the institution and propel it to the next level. If this practice persists in digital banks, it will hinder the full realization of their benefits. Bangladesh Bank (BB) could play a role in addressing this issue by imposing restrictions on the number of family members who can serve on a Digital Bank's Board of Directors and Top Executive Committee. The central bank could also implement fitness-for-duty examinations for key management positions and develop other procedures to ensure competent and professional management for digital banks (Hossain, 2021).

The availability of paved roads and electricity has had a transformative effect on the culture and economy of rural Bangladesh. Rural areas are witnessing the emergence of various urban establishments, such as coffee shops, community centers, beauty parlors, workshops for expanding rural transportation and agricultural equipment, and mobile accessory stores. This transformation is turning the rural environment into a mini-urban area. Currently, over 60 percent of rural income comes from nonfarming activities. Enhanced banking and digital financial services have facilitated the rapid flow of money from metropolitan regions and foreign countries into rural areas, making rural Bangladesh an attractive hub for commercial development. The provision of electricity in rural areas has not only alleviated the challenges of rural living but has also fostered the growth of micro, small, and medium-sized businesses, many of which are owned and operated by women. Microfinance institutions have also played a significant role in empowering rural communities as part of the rural transformation process. Digital connectivity, in particular, has been instrumental in spreading technology and urban lifestyles to rural areas (Rahman, 2022b).

Mobile banking is an evolutionary stage in India's banking system, where banks collaborate with mobile carriers to provide cutting-edge financial services across various business domains. This innovative platform of mobile banking has facilitated commercial transactions for Sri Lankan companies, offering convenience and efficiency (Kahandawa & Wijayanayake, 2014). Similarly, Nepalese individuals have found banking operations more convenient through mobile banking, thanks to its swift transactions and easy accessibility (Shrestha, 2013). A study conducted in China in 2005 explored public opinion on mobile banking and revealed that despite its numerous advantages,

Chinese individuals initially hesitated to adopt mobile banking due to security concerns (Laforet & Li, 2005). In Kenya, the cost of mobile banking emerged as a significant concern alongside security (Achieng & Ingari, 2015). In Finland, where security and reliability were paramount, compatibility, complexity, and comparative advantage also influenced the acceptance of mobile banking services among the population (Mattila, 2003).

In the context of Bangladesh, mobile banking has also been a subject of research, particularly in understanding the factors driving the adoption of mobile banking in emerging nations (Jahan & Shahria, 2021). The reasons behind consumers' shift from conventional banks to mobile banking services were investigated by Zubayer et al. (2019). The study surveyed 150 mobile banking users of various ages, educational backgrounds, and professions to understand their perspectives on the appealing aspects of mobile banking. The aim was to identify and highlight the key factors influencing the decision of Bangladeshis to adopt mobile banking. However, the study had certain limitations, including an unbalanced distribution of respondents, limited time and resources for data collection, and issues with the order of survey items, which resulted in some confusion among participants. Furthermore, respondents sometimes mixed up the availability variable with other differentiating factors, which researchers subsequently had to merge during data analysis. Nevertheless, the study provided valuable insights. It revealed that the availability of mobile banking services significantly influences the decision to switch to mobile banking or the frequency of its usage, making it the most critical factor in the adoption process. The market is predominantly dominated by bKash, a major player that has achieved substantial success through strategic moves and effective marketing. The second-place holder, DBBL, has a much smaller market share. The study also highlighted that the remaining mobile banking providers are relatively small. However, one of the study's main limitations is that the majority of respondents were university graduates with limited mobile banking needs, which does not accurately represent the diverse range of mobile phone and banking service users. Therefore, future research could be expanded to include users from different professions, particularly businesspeople and service providers. Undoubtedly, the increasing number of mobile phones has a significant impact on the growing mobile banking industry. Other influential factors, such as personal discretionary income growth and population expansion, also play a substantial role in individuals' intentions to switch to mobile banking. The study emphasized that the most crucial aspect, as identified by the researchers, is the availability of mobile banking services. The majority of respondents cited the convenience of conducting transactions anytime and anywhere as the primary reason for utilizing mobile banking.

Islam et al. (2019) conducted an analysis of the factors influencing customers' mobile banking experiences in Bangladesh and identified five factors associated with the Bangladeshi mobile banking experience. These factors include the ease of use and speed of the system, transaction precision and effectiveness, reliability, transaction security within the ATM booth, and technical problems. Confirmatory factor analysis (CFA) was used to validate these five variables. The study investigated the impact of a fast and responsive platform, transaction precision and efficiency, reliability, secure transactions in ATM booths, and technological complexity on overall customer satisfaction with mobile banking. The results indicate a strong and positive correlation between customers' overall experience with mobile banking and the convenience and responsiveness of the system, transaction precision and efficiency, and security in ATM booths. In Bangladesh, dependability and technological challenges have a minimal influence on overall customer satisfaction with mobile banking. The study also revealed gender disparities among the respondents. Male respondents prioritize characteristics such as the convenience and responsiveness of the system, transaction speed and accuracy, and secure transactions in ATM booths. Dependability and technological complexity are not crucial factors for male consumers of mobile banking in Bangladesh. On the other hand, female respondents consider transaction security within ATM booths as essential, while attributes such as efficiency and responsiveness, transaction speed and accuracy, reliability, and technological complexity hold less significance for them. It is important to note that the study only focused on mobile banking users from nine commercial banks in Bangladesh. Therefore, further research that includes a broader range of institutions and clients is necessary to obtain more precise results.

Islam et al. (2017) propose a framework for analyzing customers' behavioral intentions to adopt mobile banking in Bangladesh. Despite the popularity of mobile banking among customers, there has been limited development in this area. Therefore, it is crucial to identify the factors that influence customers' adoption of mobile banking in Bangladesh. The proposed framework extends the Unified Theory of Acceptance and Use of Technology (UTAUT) model by incorporating two additional factors: perceived trustworthiness and personal innovativeness. Although this framework has not yet been empirically tested, empirical studies are necessary to validate its applicability. Managers and bankers can utilize this framework to examine their customers' behavioral intentions to use mobile banking services. While the UTAUT theory was designed to assess the adoption of general information technology, specific technologies require a tailored approach. For instance, UTAUT may not address all the unique challenges associated with customer adoption of mobile banking services. Therefore, this study expands upon the UTAUT model by incorporating two critical characteristics specific to the mobile banking industry.

According to Bangladesh Bank and the University of Dhaka (2017), the service quality of Bangladesh's MFS sector is high. However, the analysis reveals that there is still significant room for improvement in various dimensions of MFS in Bangladesh. The MFS sector in Bangladesh faces challenges such as illicit money transfers from overseas, inadequate network systems, exploitation by criminals, and high service prices. Resolving these issues promptly would provide a substantial boost to the sector. Additionally, it is crucial for the various stakeholders in Bangladesh to understand mobile banking services and their contribution to the country's economy. Conducting further research in this area would inform the development of strategies by policymakers to foster the growth of the MFS industry. This report serves as a valuable resource for all relevant parties. It is highly recommended that ongoing research be conducted in order to keep the Bangladeshi MFS sector and its stakeholders up-to-date with the latest insights and developments.

Rahman et al. (2016) conducted a study to investigate the factors influencing the adoption of mobile banking (m-banking) in remote areas of Bangladesh, aiming to identify the underlying issues. The researchers found that perceived simplicity of use, trust, and utility had a positive impact on m-banking adoption in rural Bangladesh, while the user interface had a negative effect. These findings have significant policy implications for bank managers seeking to enhance their strategies for promoting financial inclusion and successful banking in rural areas of Bangladesh. In a literature review focused on mobile banking adoption in Jordan, the researchers defined several variables that influence the adoption process. The study revealed that all six parameters – self-efficacy, tangibility, compatibility, risk, complexity, and relative advantage – have an influence on Jordanian clients' adoption of mobile banking services. These statistics highlight the importance of considering these factors when designing and implementing mobile banking initiatives in Jordan.

According to Liza (2014), the integration of banking services and mobile technologies allows customers to perform banking transactions conveniently and securely anytime and anywhere through mobile banking. This study examines the factors driving mobile banking adoption in Bangladesh, with a focus on trust, perceived threat, perceived cost, performance risk, social risk, time risk, and financial risk. Various factors influence people's adoption of mobile banking. Convenience emerges as a key factor based on the criteria considered in this study. The findings indicate that perceived utility has a substantial impact on mobile banking adoption. When individuals recognize the value and benefits of mobile banking, they are more likely to use it. Current users of mobile banking perceive it as helpful and easy to use. There is a positive correlation between perceived usefulness and perceived ease of use, indicating that the more convenient mobile banking is, the more valuable it becomes. Therefore, it is crucial to provide banking services with useful functionality and mobile devices with user-friendly screens and input devices. Mobile banking is gaining traction in low-income countries, presenting opportunities for providers to capture a significant market share by offering essential products. This study effectively identifies the characteristics that influence the adoption of mobile banking in the low-income market.

The objective of Sharma and Hossain's (2015) study is to examine the socioeconomic impact of mobile banking in rural Bangladesh and understand the perspectives of the rural population regarding these new financial developments. Similar to many other developing countries, a large portion of the Bangladeshi population lacks access to formal banking services. While only 15 percent of adults have bank accounts, 74 percent of individuals own mobile phones. In an effort to promote financial inclusion, the government allowed twenty-eight banks to offer mobile banking services, with nineteen institutions currently providing this service. Mobile banking has gained rapid popularity in Bangladesh due to its convenient transaction capabilities. Both urban and rural residents are utilizing this technology to transfer money, receive wages, and pay bills without the need to visit a physical bank branch. Since its introduction in 2011 by two private banks, mobile banking services have successfully brought many unbanked individuals in rural areas into the formal banking system. According to Bangladesh Bank, over three million people are now using various mobile banking services, with approximately 70,000 service locations available to customers. Daily transactions through mobile banking in the country exceed USD 32 million, positioning Bangladesh as the fifth-largest provider of mobile banking services globally. Mobile banking transactions account for 5.6 percent of the country's gross domestic product, as reported by another source. The increasing adoption of mobile banking has sparked optimism among academics and policymakers, who believe it will drive economic development and reduce inequality across the nation. As Bangladesh is primarily an agricultural country with 70 percent of its population residing in rural areas, the progress of mobile banking is dependent on rural residents. Through grounded theory and semi-structured interviews with fifty mobile banking customers in a village setting, this study concludes that mobile banking has a positive impact on the socioeconomic development of rural Bangladesh. It promotes employment and entrepreneurship while reducing reliance on informal financial channels, which carry risks of data loss, fraud, and corruption. The survey also highlights that rural residents embrace mobile banking due to its convenience and speed. However, a notable proportion of individuals express concerns about the trustworthiness of mobile banking, citing fraudulent activities by certain mobile bank agents.

In Bangladesh, Khan and Chaipoopirutana (2020) conducted a study to explore the factors influencing users' behavioral intentions to use mobile technology for financial services. The research reveals that overall user satisfaction enhances the perceived utility of mobile banking services. However, in the context of Bangladesh, perceived ease of use, utility, and security have minimal impact on behavioral intentions to reuse digital money services. Except for perceived financial cost and trust, all other variables including perceived effectiveness, user satisfaction, safety, risk perception, social influence, and facilitating conditions significantly influence behavioral intentions to continue using digital money services in Bangladesh. This study addresses critical aspects identified in the literature within the specific context of Bangladesh. Previous research has primarily focused on the behavioral intentions of banking clients toward traditional mobile banking services in Bangladesh. However, this study specifically aims to explore relevant aspects of utilizing nontraditional mobile banking services such as bKash, Rocket, Nagad, and similar services that are gaining popularity in the country's financial sector. The study investigates the factors influencing the decisions of both financial and nonconsumers to use mobile banking services for digital transactions. The findings indicate that behavioral intentions to reuse mobile financial services in Bangladesh are influenced by perceived utility, ease of use, safety, perceived risk, social influence, and facilitating factors. However, behavioral intentions toward reusing mobile banking services in Bangladesh are not influenced by the perceived financial cost. Privacy positively impacts the resumption of bKash mobile banking services in Bangladesh. Bangladeshi users exhibit a strong awareness of their spending and financial habits. They perceive the security of a physical banking system to be more prominent compared to a mobile banking system, while support is more readily available. Consequently, enhanced security assurance may encourage newer and returning customers to utilize mobile banking services. The perceived risk instrument used in this study yielded a favorable interpretation, suggesting a favorable perception of the service provider.

Barua and Aker (2021) conducted a study to understand customers' perceptions of the quality of e-banking services in Bangladesh and identified the key challenges and necessary measures to promote e-banking. The findings indicate that e-banking offers various benefits, including risk reduction through quick and easy access to information, fast transactions, prompt service delivery, accuracy, effectiveness, security, and convenient banking services available anytime and anywhere. However, the survey also reveals critical issues affecting Bangladesh's e-banking services, including technological disruptions, inadequate infrastructure, limited-service availability in rural areas, and high service charges. Customers identified technological disruption as the primary obstacle to implementing an e-banking system. Inadequate infrastructure ranked second, followed by the lack of access to services in remote regions. Slow internet connection response and occasional failures in internet connectivity disrupt the e-banking system. Moreover, the lack of up-to-date and innovative IT resources and insufficient power backup continue to affect the efficiency of Bangladesh's e-banking system. Customers expressed reluctance toward online banking due to the high cost of services, hidden charges, and the complexity of the operational system. Consequently, expensive service charges and system complexity were ranked as the fourth and fifth challenges, respectively. However, customers considered a lack of knowledge and significant investments in automation and maintenance to be the least of their concerns when implementing an e-banking system.

In the next phase of development, technology will play a crucial role in enhancing efficiency by reducing production time and costs. The government's objective is to establish a digital Bangladesh, although the desired level of advancement has not yet been achieved. To keep pace with rapid technological progress and bridge the digital divide, substantial investment is necessary to ensure affordable access to technology. The increasing inequality poses a hindrance to the country's progress. Despite the growth in GDP and per capita income, income disparity has also escalated. The significant wealth gap contradicts the principles of independence and the constitution, which advocate for an equitable society (Khatun, 2022). Bangladesh's ICT services industry holds significant potential for growth, fueled by a large pool of educated young individuals with software development skills. The country's aim to become a developed nation through the expansion of the ICT sector has been prioritized by the government under Vision 2021. Considerable progress has been made in improving access to ICT services. This program is crucial for increasing technological access among the population and fostering domestic demand for IT services (UNCTAD, 2016).

To sustain the current trajectory of economic development, it is imperative to enhance the efficiency of public services and bureaucracy. Improving the skills of public service providers is vital for better service delivery. Citizens should have the convenience of tracking their files and receiving updates without the need to visit government offices. Streamlining processes, such as automatically processing and providing licenses within a specified timeframe, is essential. Although progress has been made, further improvements in business facilitation are necessary to accelerate development. The public sector should strive for parity with the private sector by eliminating bureaucratic complications and ensuring swift decision-making and implementation (Khatun, 2022).

2.4 Analytical Framework of the Study

We are currently experiencing the fourth industrial revolution, characterized by the automation of machines without human intervention. As technology evolves, client expectations have reached unprecedented levels. Service providers that can adapt to the changing needs of their clients will thrive in the market. This reality applies to banking and financial institutions as well. Open banking, the platform of the future generation, is rapidly replacing traditional banking concepts. The rise of fintech companies offering financial services will contribute to the growth of open banking. Ultimately, the combination of open banking and fintech firms will reshape the perception of traditional banking and provide clients with a new and enhanced financial services experience (Islam, 2022).

The COVID-19 pandemic has brought about an unprecedented global crisis. It has profoundly influenced various aspects of people's lives, such as work patterns, payment methods, shopping habits, and financial transactions. Safety has become a paramount concern for conscientious individuals. In this context, mobile banking has emerged as a viable option for providing individuals with convenient and secure access to financial services. With the advent of the digital world, traditional banking practices in Bangladesh are becoming obsolete. The rapid adoption of digital banking and the strength of MFSs will soon render physical cash counters unnecessary for banks. While financial transactions are infrequent in rural areas, MFS providers have successfully connected the underserved residents of these regions to the formal financial system (Khatun et al., 2021).

The analytical framework (in Figure 1) employed in this study encompasses both independent and dependent variables. Through an analysis of the concepts of mobile banking and its progression, as well as a review of relevant literature, the framework was developed to understand the factors influencing mobile banking adoption and its impact.

2.4.1 Independent Variables

2.4.1.1 Perceived Usefulness

The degree of perceived usefulness under which a person believes that utilizing a given system will improve their job prospects. The level to which consumers believe that using a given service will be painless is denoted to as perceived ease of use. As a result, good-faith assessments of m-government services could be

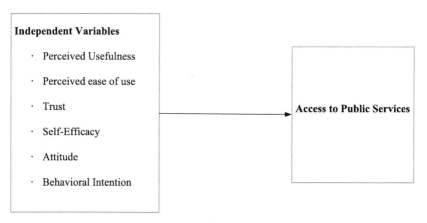

Figure 1 Analytical framework.

Source: Analytical Framework developed by the authors based on Akhter & Khalily, 2020; Bangladesh Bank, 2019; BCC, 2011; Ehsan et al., 2019; Himel et al., 2021; Hossain & Haque, 2014; Islam et al., 2017; Islam et al., 2019; Khan & Chaipoopirutana, 2020; Khatun et al., 2021; Liza, 2014; Rahman et al., 2016; Zubayer et al. 2019.

based either on mobile communication effectiveness or on understandable mobile communication content (Bampo et al., 2008; Prins & Verhoef, 2007). The assumption that using technology would improve the quality of one's work is referred to as perceived usefulness. The employment of a particular platform would allow users to achieve enhanced levels of performance, efficacy, and productivity when performing a specific task, which was characterized as a perceived utility.

2.4.1.2 Trust

Trust suggests that the other gathering will behave in a predictable and socially responsible manner, therefore meeting the innocent party's expectations (Warkentin et al., 2002). Trust is evident as the idea that different parties would not act unethically and that transaction providers will deliver on their promises. Trust means that the user is confident in its expertise, integrity, and goodwill when it comes to mobile financial services. Additionally, people are more inclined to use e-government tools if they believe the government has the necessary knowledge to design and secure e-government services (Carter & Weerakkody, 2008). Users' trust in mobile communication may influence their willingness to adopt a positive attitude. The importance of improving service communication content in building trust has been emphasized (Gefen et al., 2003).

2.4.1.3 Self-Efficacy

Self-efficacy describes a person's technological understanding (Seo & Bernsen, 2016). It is distinct as the belief that one can effectively carry out a specific action (Bandura, 1997). Both characteristics influence the perceived behavior controller, which is described as an individual's of how easy or hard it is to complete a specific activity (Ajzen, 1991). Self-efficacy might thus contribute to behavioral control through a user's mobile announcement. Studies also show that interpersonal influence impacts service communication (Gallivan et al., 2005).

2.4.1.4 Attitude

Attitude mentions to an individual's positive or negative feelings toward achieving a goal (Davis, 1989). Perspectives in involuntary contexts, such as e-commerce, e-banking, mobile banking, and e-government, are strongly linked to behavior intention (Al-Debei et al., 2013). As a result, a user's attitude is predicted to forecast their actual desire to use e-services.

2.4.1.5 Behavioral Intention

The decision to engage in exact conduct is influenced by the preferences and opinions of others (Ajzen, 1991). As a result, critical viewpoints may influence user preferences (Bhattacherjee & Sanford, 2006). Interpersonal influence affects one's proclivity toward engaging in or forsaking a particular activity, and one's level of participation in that activity is determined as just a consequence (Montoya et al., 2010). The social context impacts e-government acceptance (Shareef et al., 2011), including peer influence explaining individual preferences for e-government service. The intention of such a consumer to remain using a product, and lower and increase the volume of service received from a previously experienced service provider is known as reuse intention.

2.4.2 Dependent Variable

2.4.2.1 Access to Public Services

"Public services" refers to the diverse range of services provided to residents by local, state, and national governments (European Commission, 2010). In the context of a public resource, the term "public service" refers to services such as postal service, railroads, roads, and others, where signal quality, operational efficiency, and a supply chain that ensures universal access are key criteria for success (Syvertsen, 1999). The concept of public services encompasses various aspects of the public sphere. This is significant because it implies that our approach should be guided by political processes and the policies they generate, rather than relying solely on the certainty of economic theory. This interplay between the political and economic spheres lies at the core of the evolving political framework of social services worldwide (Martin, 2004). In this study, the dependent variable is access to public services. Access to public services is determined by factors such as perceived utility, convenience, self-efficacy, trust, attitude, and behavioral intention. These factors influence individuals' ability to avail themselves of public services effectively.

2.5 Conclusion

The banking sector has undergone a significant transformation, moving away from the traditional model of customers waiting in line to a technology-driven approach that allows transactions to be conducted anytime and anywhere, as long as individuals have network connectivity to access their respective banks' services. The introduction of mobile banking has led to explosive growth in the global banking industry, including India (Balakrishnan & Sudha, 2016). In developing countries like Bangladesh, digital technologies such as mobile banking have the potential to greatly enhance financial access for the population (Khatun et al., 2021). With a large and relatively young population, Bangladesh presents ample opportunities for innovative entrepreneurs and investors. To foster innovation, collaboration among the mobile sector, the broader internet ecosystem, and the government is crucial. This collaboration can involve initiatives such as supporting the development of incubators, making application programming interfaces (APIs) available to local start-ups, and bridging the funding gap through venture capital funds that invest in seed-stage start-ups (GSMA, 2018).

Bangladesh's financial system comprises formal, semi-formal, and informal sectors, with the formal sector being dominant. Historically, the country's financial system was primarily governed by state-owned banks until the 1980s (Batten et al., 2015). Presently, the banking industry in Bangladesh consists of six state-owned commercial banks, three state-owned specialized banks primarily engaged in development finance, forty-two private commercial banks, and nine foreign commercial banks. Research shows that only 36 percent of individuals have access to formal financial services, while 43 percent have access to quasi-formal financing. Many people in Bangladesh, especially smallholder farmers and low-income workers, still lack access to formal financial sources due to factors such as illiteracy, collateral requirements, and lengthy loan processing procedures. Various obstacles, including financial illiteracy, lack of awareness, attitudes of bank employees, limited physical access, high costs, insufficient initiatives by banks and financial institutions, and inadequate technology infrastructure, impede access to financial services in Bangladesh. Lack of access to finance hampers agriculture and business investments. To address these challenges, the introduction of ATMs, agent banking, internet banking, and mobile banking can offer potential solutions and play an active role in facilitating financial access for the population in Bangladesh (Khatun et al., 2021).

This study utilized primary data to examine the status of mobile banking and its impact on enhancing financial access in Bangladesh. While mobile banking gained popularity in the country in 2011, customer acceptance has grown steadily in subsequent years, providing a simple, quick, and secure means of financial access. The COVID-19 pandemic has further accelerated the adoption of mobile banking as people prioritize hygiene and aim to prevent the spread of the virus. Consequently, there has been a significant increase in the number of registered mobile banking customers during the outbreak. Mobile banking transactions, including cash-out, cash-in, and peer-to-peer transactions, have experienced disruptions due to the pandemic but have also witnessed significant growth as people shift toward digital transactions and government initiatives (Khatun et al., 2021). Mobile banking has become increasingly beneficial for tasks such as recharge, remittance transactions, contribution delivery, and distribution of safety net funds. The entire section is finally able to provide a structure of analysis. The next sections will focus on the analysis part.

3 Present Scenario of Mobile Banking in Bangladesh

3.1 Introduction

Recent advances in communications have permitted the introduction of new financial access methods, including mobile banking, in which a consumer connects with a bank through a mobile phone (Barnes & Corbitt, 2003). In the early twenty-first century, the mobile phone was the first communiqué device to gain popularity in developing nations such as Bangladesh. With the convergence of the two greatest recent technical developments – the Internet and the mobile phone – a new service (mobile data service) is established, and the banking business conducts its first wireless internet commercial transaction (Barnes & Corbitt, 2003).

Bangladesh's banking system has been unable to withstand technological encroachment as a result of the persistent rise of an economy driven by information. The recurring growth and modernization of banking patterns have been prompted by the demand for quick access to financial resources beyond customary rules. And given the enormous demand for finance-related services, institutions other than traditional banks have entered the race in an effort to seize the perceived opportunity inside the banking industry (Islam, 2013). Mobile banking is among the most current financial services, delivering some of the most important banking procedures to the pockets of consumers. The demand for this new financial service is expanding daily alongside the global proliferation of cell phones. Because of the current state of affairs, financial institutions such as banks, software companies, microfinance institutions, and network operators can now provide this novel service alongside digital products and services meant to increase their client base (including financially excluded populations), boost consumer loyalty, broaden their market share, and generate new job openings (Shaikh, 2013). Even so, much like in many other least-developed and developing countries, 80 percent of the people in Bangladesh motionless does not have admittance to safe and sound financial services. Roughly half of all individuals have a conventional bank account (Alam & Sarowar, 2020), requiring the majority of people to trust alternate financial organizations with high fees, so keeping unbanked in a sequence of poverty (Parvez et al., 2015).

Instead, 97 percent of people in the nation own a mobile phone, prompting officials to capitalize on this potential by introducing mobile banking services. As the part of government's financial presence initiative, the central bank permitted twenty-eight banks to offer mobile banking; sixteen have thus far complied (Sharma et al., 2022). Bangladeshis have rapidly embraced mobile banking as a result of their convenient transaction choices. People in both urban and rural regions use this innovative technology to transmit money, get earnings, pay bills, and check their stability, transactional data, and other bank activities via their smartphones at any time and from any location, without being required to visit a bank office. Experts and representatives believe that the rising usage of mobile banking will contribute to the nation's economic growth and overall inequality reduction (Rahman, 2014). Commercial banking has been shown in several studies to have the possibility of increasing the availability of financial offerings to low-income people who are currently not attended by traditional banks. This is since the cost of distribution, which comprises both the cost for banks to set up and maintain a distribution strategy and the cost for customers to try to gain access to services, is reduced (Ivatuary & Mas, 2010).

"Connecting citizens in meaningful ways" is one of the primary objectives of Digital Bangladesh. As in the majority of emerging economies, Bangladesh's internet access is predominantly mobile due to a lack of fixed-line substructure; just 3.8 percent of the population subscribes to fixed wideband services associated with 51 percent mobile infiltration. By connecting devices, mobile operators are exclusively situated to play a significant role in the growth of digital societies, with the availability of devices, wireless services, and content promoting digital inclusion and bridging the digital divide, thereby contributing to Bangladesh's goal of becoming a middle-income nation. Consequently, mobile technology plays a crucial role in achieving the SDGs and Vision 2021 goals in Bangladesh (GSMA, 2018). Around the world, mobile banking is expanding at a breakneck pace. The process creates a lot of confusion about how the government should respond to this new service. New electronic channels are replacing traditional television channels. Mobile devices are a relatively recent phenomenon in the dissemination of electronic services. To improve business services and marketing methods and tell academics about promising future study fields (Ahmed et al., 2012). Customers can undertake various financial activities without having access to conventional banks thanks to financial services offered through mobile networks that are completed by mobile phone or digital help. It is becoming a hot topic in the financial industry. It is a collection of procedures that enables bank customers to access bank services via mobile phone, ranging from an essential handset to digital help. Mobile banking services have become more important components of just doing business, including implementing company strategies for economic growth in recent years (Dona et al., 2014).

Despite the fact that Bangladesh's economy is undergoing industrialization as a result of its continuous transition from agriculture to industry and services, the country remains strongly dependent on agriculture and confronts substantial food insecurity and production issues. In the future, ongoing population expansion, uncontrolled urbanization, and natural catastrophes may worsen these problems. As one of the most weather patterns countries in the world, Bangladesh's coping and adaptation issues will be exacerbated by climate change, as will larger socioeconomic challenges. Vision 2021 is the geopolitical vision as to where Bangladesh wants to be on the fiftieth anniversary of its liberation – which demonstrates the government of Bangladesh's progressive development plan in awareness of the necessity to overcome these difficulties. The primary objective is for Bangladesh to attain a middle-income status and eradicate poverty. A fundamental part of Vision 2021 is "Digital Bangladesh," an initiative with the goal of fostering socioeconomic development via the use of ICT (GSMA, 2018). The idea of the digital gap derives from the comparative phenomena of many types of inequality and seeks to provide relevant insights regarding the spectrum of separate internet access and online abilities (i.e., the first- and second-level digital divides) in Bangladesh. Although internet access became obtainable in Bangladesh in the early 1990s, it progressed slowly until 2008, when just 0.4 percent of the population accessed the Internet. Contempt the introduction of mobile internet in 2005, Bangladesh did not experience an increase in internet access or procedure during this time period. Nonetheless, between 2009 and 2011, 3.5 percent of the population arrived in the Internet domain. This was the result of a considerable reduction in the prices of internet-capable mobile phones and internet service consumption (Siddiquee & Islam, 2020).

Microelectronic payment technologies are rapidly displacing traditional payment methods. Online financial transactions involving some digital financial equipment are required for electronic payment systems. They have enabled the government, corporations, and banking institutions to provide their clients with various payment options. Charge account credit, mobile banking, master card, automatic teller machines, and bill payments via mobile are some of the payment options available (Kumar, 2022). Multinational banks have long operated in Bangladesh, and there are numerous nationalized, private commercial, and specialty banks. International banks are supposed to provide superior service. Some banks have launched mobile banking services to improve their performance (Hossain & Haque, 2014). Online financial transactions involving some digital financial equipment are required for electronic payment systems. They have enabled the government, corporations, and banking institutions to provide their clients with various payment options. Charge account credit, mobile banking, master card, automatic teller machines, and bill payments via mobile are some of the payment options available. MFS played a critical role in today's online companies and other financial and commercial services in a fast-paced and pandemic world.

3.2 Digital Banking for Bangladesh

Prior to 2010, banks had an important role in the monetary system, but they were unable to significantly advance their financial presence. Since 2011, the trend based on mobile financial services has advanced considerably. As a result of the widespread use of cutting-edge technology, the financial industry is undergoing profound changes. Undoubtedly, the financial sector will become more technology-focused or -oriented. As long as legislative limitations do not preclude them from doing so, several technology-based fintech firms may and will provide services to multiple operators in order to achieve a critical mass through technology and retail networks. Every industry will undergo transformation and evolution. These changes are occurring to provide consumers with a better experience, new and creative goods, and more diversity. The ultimate objectives are to reduce costs, enhance ease, and facilitate service to diverse customer groups. In addition, as consumers' demands, expectations, and behaviors evolve, technology is increasingly used to monitor and adapt to their evolving requirements (Hossain, 2021).

Offering services through digital channels enables service providers to collect and keep data about client behavior in order to analyze their requirements and deliver lifestyle or business-specific financial services. The notion, along with other benefits such as operational efficiency and cost savings, is encouraging enterprises to adopt digital services to better serve their consumers. The banking sector is no exception; in order to satisfy the evolving expectations of customers, the mentality of banking sector employees must adapt. Customers of banks are increasingly desiring digital offerings. As a result, the banking system (particularly private banking) is already undergoing significant evolutionary and transformational processes. The next step in the evolution of banks is referred to as "Digital Banks" (Hossain, 2021).

3.3 Mobile Financial Services Overview

The rapid spread of mobile phones all across the industrialized regions is one of the most remarkable technological advancements of the previous decade. Prepaid cards and low-priced phones have enabled hundreds of millions of first-time telephone users to incorporate voice calls and text messaging into their daily lives. Notwithstanding, many of these new mobile users reside in structured or income economies and lack access to the banking services that others consider normal. There are potentially more consumers with mobile phones than checking accounts in the emerging nation (Porteous, 2006). Various efforts deliver financial services to "the unbanked" using mobile phones. These services take different forms, such as long-distance remittance, micropayments, and familiar airtime trading systems, and are known by numerous names, such as mobile transfers, mobile banking, and mobile banking. Collectively, they are no longer pilots; in the Philippines, Kenya, South Africa, and other countries, these services are widely accessible and gaining popularity (Dona et al., 2014).

Millions of individuals in developing nations depend on informal economic activity and local-level networks for their livelihoods. The majority of these groups are from the base of the pyramid, and they lack access to fundamental financial services/banks due to their prohibitive cost and restricted availability. Nevertheless, the phenomenal rise of the mobile industry globally has made it possible to offer social and financial services over the mobile network. It is currently a pressing concern in financial services. It is a standardized set of procedures that enables bank clients to access bank services through mobile phones, beginning with a basic mobile handset and progressing to personal digital help. Today, mobile banking services are vital workings of doing business and executing a corporate strategy for economic growth (Dona et al., 2014). Some banks are making substantial reserves in mobile technologies to generate a variety of business values, ranging from higher competence and cost decrease to enhanced operational performance and customer service for a competitive edge. The expanded obtainability and performance of mobile communications infrastructure throughout the world have contributed to this growth. The number of mobile device varieties has increased significantly, and their capacity has also increased. The lowering prices of data transmission and the lowering costs of smartphones as a result of providers' intense competition have expedited the proliferation of communication devices and the development of the international mobile market. In nations with underdeveloped traditional communications infrastructure, mobile technologies are revolutionizing the accessibility of internet-based services. Mobile banking is the modern channel in electronic banking that facilitates the performance of banking transactions via mobile phones and other mobile devices. As there are several times as many mobile phone users as online PC users, the possibility for mobile banking may be far bigger than for outmoded desktop banking. Increasing "mobile lifestyles" may also contribute to the expansion of everywhere, all the time apps (Shah & Clarke, 2009). Low costs, minimal time consumption, privacy, independence from time and location, and simple communication are factors that influence the utilization of technology. The use of a mobile phone for banking purposes has been hindered by a growing number of influences, counting perceived trustworthiness and security concerns (Luarn & Lin, 2005).

Bangladesh has set a long-term objective of becoming a developed nation by 2041. Bangladesh has also pledged to meet the Sustainable Development Goals (SDGs) by 2030. With this broad vision in mind, the Bangladesh government had also prioritized facilitating access to quality financial services for all individuals and businesses to balance the financial sector's inclusiveness and depth and the variety of the development plan. Due to the disturbance of the "Digital Bangladesh" undertaking with huge financial sector advancement, Bangladesh is becoming a leading expert in financial intermediation. A well-known name in microfinance with a notable achievement in using digital finance is to promote mobile financial services. Bangladesh's government views finance as a powerful tool for comprehensive growth or shared prosperity.

According to available evidence, financial services have a substantial positive impact on homebound and professional sociocultural connections, and access to finance is seen as important for reducing poverty in Bangladesh. Financial assets, banking liabilities, and loans have steadily increased in the last few decades. This country's financial system has proven to be rather stable and unshakable. The financial sector has undergone significant changes over this time, particularly in reaction to the ongoing transformations, including changes in the structure of the actual economy (Kumar, 2022). Several technical, organizational, and regulatory hurdles impede the growth of e-banking in Bangladesh, including a lack of dependable and secured communications technologies and a backbone network covering the entire country. Low ICT penetration in the banking sector, a shortage of experienced workers and training facilities, and e-transaction-friendly policy initiatives, guidelines, laws, and regulatory requirements. Despite the obstacles, Bangladesh Bank's attempts to modernize the country's payment system, as well as the government's goal to develop a "Digital Bangladesh," have created rivalry among scheduled institutions to improve financial services and implement e-banking on a larger scale (Ahmed et al., 2012). Utility payment systems, merchant payments, contributions into bank savings accounts or schemes, and person-to-company expenses include loan repayments of banks, nonbank financial companies, and microfinance groups, including insurance premium payments to insurance firms (Rahman, 2015). BKash, Rocket, UKash, MyCash, and SureCash are among the thirteen banks now offering mobile banking services in the nation, as reported by the central bank. They offer money transfers, cash-in, cash-outs, salary distribution, donations for the needy, stipend disbursements, remittances, payments for various government services, toll payments, credit card bill repayments, and insurance premiums (Modak, 2022).

Following the execution of financial sector reform initiatives and the introduction of new technologies over the past two decades, Bangladesh's financial services businesses have experienced extraordinary branch development, innovation, viability, competitiveness, and profitability. Despite this development, there are worries that banks have not been able to provide basic financial services to a substantial helping of the population, particularly the disadvantaged and rural residents. Lack of shortest access to financial organizations and acceptable products, high operative expenses, and hazards stemming from asymmetries in information are the primary causes for the exclusion of a substantial number of individuals. The financial industry must create more cost-effective methods to provide personalized goods to the unbanked poor. Instead of establishing a standard branch, which is not always possible due to high costs, mobile technology may be beneficial in serving the poor by decreasing the cost of operation finished the use of low-cost technology channels. Bangladesh has millions of mobile phone users and a larger coverage area of Mobile Network Operators (MNO), which are now employed as an alternate distribution channel for providing mobile financial services to the unbanked/ banked populations. This section will evaluate the growing presentation and potential of mobile financial services in Bangladesh as a supporter of ethical banking (Nabi et al., 2017). In April of 2022, financial transactions revolving around Eid-ul-Fitr accounted for BDT 107,460 billion in the most transactions. According to statistics from Bangladesh Bank, mobile financial transactions in May 2022 amounted to BDT 76,312 billion, which is fewer than typical levels. As Eid-ul-Fitr happened at the very beginning of May, according to officials from several MFS providers, the majority of festival-related transactions, including bonuses and purchasing, occurred in the previous month (Modak, 2022).

Due to financial industry reform and technology adaptation, Bangladesh has seen tremendous progress in retail banking, sustainability, successful operations, service design, and worldwide competitive mode. Despite this progress, this same vast majority of people, particularly the poor and all those living in rural areas, remain unable to access a variety of financial services due to a lack of traditional financial institutions, a lack of higher service charges, appropriate economic initiatives, and also insufficient data (Kabir et al., 2020). After Bangladesh acquired independence in 1971, the country's banking industry began with six national commercial banks, and three state-owned specialized banks, including nine international banks. The banking industry made a huge step forward in the 1980s with the advent of private banks. There have two kinds of banks in Bangladesh. Firstly, the Bangladesh Bank Order of 1972 and the Bank Company Act of 1991 allow sixty-one approved banks in Bangladesh to operate under Bangladesh's immediate supervision and ultimate authority (Bangladesh Bank).

Bangladesh has developed a paradigm headed by banks to provide mobile financial services (the other model is the telephone company-led model, telco model in brief). Bangladesh Bank authorizes the succeeding mobile financial services (in broad categories) under 2011 strategies: (i) Transfer of incoming overseas remittances; (ii) Cash in/out via mobile accounts at agents/ATMs/bank branches/mobile operator's retail locations; (iii) Person-to-business payments (e.g., utility bills payment); (iv) Business-to-person payments (e.g., salary disbursement by industries/corporate bodies/offices); (v) Government-to-person payments (e.g., freedom-fighter allowances, elderly allowances, subsidies); (vi) Person-to-government payments (e.g., tax, levy payments); (vii) Person-to-person payments (among registered account holders of the same bank); and (viii) Other payments like microfinance, insurance premium, overdrawn facility, and DPS. In order to gain the benefits of mobile technology-based financial services, Bangladeshi banks have undertaken a number of efforts prompted by Bangladesh Bank, the country's central bank (Nabi et al., 2017). The government, including three specialty banks, owns six commercial banks. There are forty-three private business banks in Bangladesh, most held by individuals or private firms, and nine international commercial banks (FCBs) operate as scheduled banks. The second group is the nonscheduled banks: The Company Act applies to nonscheduled banks. They do not, however, follow the same schedule as Scheduled banks. These would be established to achieve specific and distinct objectives. Nonscheduled banks cannot perform all of the scheduled banks' functions. (i) Karmashangsthan Bank, (ii) Ansar VDP Unnayan Bank, (iii) Palli Sanchay Bank, (iv) Jubilee Bank, and (v) Grameen Bank are the five nonscheduled banks (Kumar, 2022). Due to the failure of conventional financial institutions to serve the poor in Bangladesh, a huge number of nongovernmental organizations have been formed to give collateral-free lending to the impoverished in Bangladesh. Yet microfinance outreach remains considerably below its potential. A huge number of poor people are excluded from formal financial services due to high operational costs and resulting interest rates, which is one of the primary obstacles to delivering financial services to the poor. Mobile financial services have created new opportunities for the underbanked. Although prominent Bangladeshi MFIs employ ICT to address concerns of top management, they trail behind in mobile microfinance initiatives. Some MFIs, such as BRAC and ASA, offer mobile financial services solely in the form of money transfers. If a more conducive atmosphere can be established, a greater number of MFIs will provide all types of mobile financial services (Nabi et al., 2017). Until 2009, Bangladesh's financial system relied solely on paper transactions. Following that, with the help of Bangladesh Bank, most private commercial banks moved the country toward an automated banking industry that met international standards. E-banking in Bangladesh offers various services, counting online banking, debit and credit card services, home banking, ATM services, online banking, telebanking, and mobile banking, among others. Even though many various e-banking channels are in use, the author of this Element has focused on e-payment, specifically using debit and credit cards (Islam et al., 2015). Table 1 displays the mobile financial services and their providers in Bangladesh.

When Bangladesh Bank established a comprehensive portable network, many transportable users and quite sound IT facilities were developed. Since launching a ubiquitous handheld network in 2011, the nation's central bank efficiently used off-branch MFS inside the country 2011. By that time, there were a lot of mobile users and quite well IT infrastructures. The concept of a bank-led MFS is quickly gaining traction (Bangladesh Bank). Bangladesh Bank licensees handle the most cash outbound and inbound, and business to person (B2P), person to company (P2B), government to person (G2P), including government to government (P2G), transfers of money. This service doesn't allow for foreign money delivery, but it will enable internal overseas

Table 1 Mobile finance service and their providers in Bangladesh.

Serial	Name of the Bank Providing MFS	Name of the Mobile Financial Service
1	Bangladesh Commerce Bank Limited	BCB Sure Cash
2	Bangladesh Post Office	Nagad
3	Bank Asia Limited	Hello
4	Brac Bank Limited	Bkash
5	Dutch Bangla Bank Limited	Rocket
6	First Security Islami Bank Limited	First Pay Sure Cash
7	Islami Bank Bangladesh Limited	mCash
8	Jamuna Bank Limited	Jamuna Bank Sure Cash
9	Meghna Bank Limited	Tap' n Pay
10	Mercantile Bank Limited	MY Cash
11	One Bank Limited	OK wallet
12	Rupali Bank Limited	Sure Cash
13	Sonali Bank Limited	Sonali e-wallet
14	Standard Bank Limited	Spot Cash
15	Trust Bank Limited	T cash
16	United Commercial Bank Limited	U cash

Source: Author's

remittances within banking channels. Any adult can open an MFS account with operators at a bank branch or agent point by submitting photographs and legal documents. It is not possible to use the same provider for multiple MFS accounts; each account belongs to a separate person.

All banks in Bangladesh have adopted the National Payment Switch (NPS), which allows a customer with valid bank documentation to withdraw money from any POS or automated teller machine (ATM) across the country, significantly cutting transaction costs. Because transactions will be directed by NPS rather than the Visa, Amex, and MasterCard networks outside of the country, they will buy and sell via web portals (Kumar, 2022). The country's eighteen MFS technicians are now offering salary disbursement, sending money, cash-in, cash-out, and donation for the poor, remittance, stipend disbursement, and payments for various government offerings. With the progress in development and digital integration, additional services include credit card bill payments, toll payments, health care premiums, and more (Hasan, 2021). Payment of utility bills is one example of

Table 2 Mobile operators and their payment services in Bangladesh.

Operator Name	Mobile Payment Services
Banglalink Digital Communications Limited	Mobile banking, train ticket, mobile cash remittance, mobile money order, post office partners.
Grameenphone Limited	Bill pay, utility bills pay, ticketing service for trains and mobicash.
Robi Axiata Limited	Robi facilities for a top-up for prepaid and postpaid customers, SMS bill payment, mobile ticketing, and Robi cash.
Teletalk Bangladesh Limited	Teletalk applied online, convenience bill, expense for BTCL subscribers, university fee process for public Universities, pay for university admission form, the registration process for HSC and SSC candidates, electricity bill expense.

Source: Author's

a micropayment system. An institution that offers utility services such as electricity, gas, water, telephone, and generator should maintain a utility bill account in such a designated bank. In this case, the network carrier acts as the intermediary, transferring funds from the customer's bank to the utility bill receiver's bank. There will be no need to use the national payment method because utility bills are micropayments, and both the customer's bank and the utility bill recipient bank should be registered with the mobile operator (Islam et al., 2015). Table 2 presents the mobile operators and a list of their payment services in Bangladesh.

The involvements of sound financial management and operation, strong customer trust, and a mature payment system are the main advantages of MFS. Banks can link consumers' cell phone numbers to their bank accounts by providing a comprehensive and flexible safety system that ensures payment security. Local banks have established mobile phone banking services with many customers at a low cost and a high degree of confidence, utilizing their account management skills. Money transfer has gone digital, with Bangladesh Bank launching an online prepaid card system with a digital payment option. Mobile phone banking services, which combine mobile communications with e-currency, provide access to financial assistance at any time and location while also expanding the banking service content. Banks may give classic and innovative services more safely and effectively (Hossain et al., 2017). Access to finance is a critical component of Bangladesh's development strategy, as a straightforward approach to finance promotes growth and reduces deficits. The prospect of introducing MFSs in Bangladesh appears promising.

Nonetheless, sufficient effort is required to extend the MFS link and system to include the outstanding unbanked people. A field examination can begin to integrate fundamental intuition in forging and resolving legal procedures for MFS. However, while more than half of Bangladesh's listed banks provide MFS, just three – BRAC Bank's bKash, Bangladesh Post Office's Nagad, and Dutch-Bangla Bank Limited's Rocket – are fully operational. Each is in charge of the region of the country with the most extensive coverage. Only a few banks are still focused on "banking," while the rest focus on "Money Transfers." Financial inclusion cannot be aided and supported by a mere "money transfer." The provider of mobile banking services should offer a variety of services in a unified wallet (account). Mobile banking providers should place a greater emphasis on credit and savings plans. MFS providers must engage rural populations to achieve true financial inclusion for economic development, as a substantial sum of money remains dormant. Bangladesh's economic improvement will be evident if idle funds are channeled into the financial system. Three new services are recommended in our proposed model. Those services, particularly the retail banking assistance we advocated, can be considered by the MFS provider. Bangladesh Bank could take the initiative to introduce those services through MFS providers, ensuring that MFS growth continues to rise and is sustained over time (Kabir et al., 2020).

3.4 Public Services and Government Initiatives

Bangladesh possesses a fast-expanding mobile financial services sector (Parvez et al., 2015). Vision and culture centered on the customer are essential for transforming government entities to better serve the public. Understanding what matters most to a broad client base is a significant obstacle for organizations attempting to scale up their service operations by maximizing the use of their time and resources. Developing a customer-centric vision and culture is necessary for transforming government entities to better serve the public. Understanding what is most important to a varied client demographic is a significant obstacle for organizations attempting to scale up their service operations by using their time and resources more effectively. Understanding customer requirements and agency capacity are crucial for resetting client expectations to a reasonable level and enhancing what service providers can offer (BIGD, 2020). A comprehensive and well-coordinated policy shift is needed to align all necessary parties, such as ministries and financial bodies. BB remains the primary anchor, however. Throughout the epidemic, it has demonstrated its competence in advancing the financial inclusion mission. It has collaborated extensively with the government and other controlling agencies in devising and executing multiple stimulus programs to mitigate the effects of the epidemic, with a particular emphasis on the attainment micro, small, and medium-sized businesses. Even while bigger companies have been better positioned to make use of these financial facilities, it appears that this inclusive funding assistance has been highly beneficial in launching a robust retrieval procedure out of the pandemic's ashes (Rahman, 2022a).

Bangladesh Bank has set a target of achieving 'financial inclusion for all by 2024' through the utilization of mobile financial services. There is a substantial possibility for expansion in this industry, as several sectors might profit from these services. Numerous measures have been made by the government to facilitate such services (LightCastle Partners, 2020). Digital Bangladesh's top aims are: (a) preparing human properties for the twenty-first century; (b) interconnecting citizens in meaningful ways; (c) bringing services to citizens' doorsteps, and (d) using digital technology to make the private market and market more competitive and productive. In all four areas of Digital Bangladesh, significant progress has been made thus far, with a special emphasis on making government services more easily accessible to residents. The Access to Information (a2i) project, which strives to improve quality, broaden access, and regionalize the delivery of public services to Bangladeshi individuals, is a primary driver of this trend. Training more than 200,000 public officials and thousands of Digital Centre Entrepreneurs to deploy e-services centrally is one of the early benefits (GSMA, 2018).

Since the global financial crisis, BB has been promoting inclusive finance with a focus on underserved parts of agriculture and SMEs for many years. The central bank also used environmentally friendly "green" output methods to support inclusive sustainable growth. BB's policy measures accorded a high priority to women entrepreneurs' access to capital. In actuality, it has been attempting to transform the real economy for those living at the base of the social pyramid. All banking, financial institutions, and clientele group stake-holders were included in the continuing education and motivating programs that kicked off the major nationwide effort to promote inclusive, green finance. Continuing as a full-fledged creativity to firmly embed socially and ecologically accountable financing into the institutional philosophy of our monetary seg-ment, the successful motivational campaigns continue to foster the enthusiastic engagement of all institutions of banking and finance –private sector and state-owned, foreign, and local (Rahman, 2022a). Since 2011, the Bangladesh Telecommunication Regulatory Commission (BTRC) has observed a definite increase trend in internet access and subscriptions. For instance, in March 2020, the number of internet subscribers – defined as those who have had at least one access in the previous 90 days – reached a new record of around 103.25 million. Furthermore, the number of people using broadband internet is mostly focused in the cities of Sylhet, Chattogram, and Dhaka and has just lately begun to spread to the district and upazila levels. Since 2011, the number of internet users in rural regions has also been rapidly increasing. With the introduction of 3G in 2013 and 4G in 2018, rural Bangladesh has already hit a milestone in terms of internet penetration – the causes behind digitization (Siddiquee & Islam, 2020).

The government has seized the opportunity presented by this expansion and implemented pro-rural policies like the establishment of Union Digital Centres (previously known as Community Information Centres), the digitization of local government institutions (LGIs) and public services, and the incorporation of ICT into the delivery of healthcare and education services. For the benefit of those living in rural Bangladesh, the government has already constructed 5,275 digital centers under such initiatives, including 4,550 Union Digital Centers (UDCs) (Islam, 2018). Nevertheless, despite the continuous rise of internet access in less than a decade and praiseworthy government measures, rural residents are not experiencing an increase in online skills and internet usage. For a better knowledge of all women, this online study investigates the first and second digital gaps that remain in rural Bangladesh. Ensuring rural people's access to and usage of the Internet is an increasing issue and a formidable problem for Bangladesh. In Bangladesh's rural areas, the government must be aware of the differences between the factors contributing to the first and second digital divides. This study aims to uncover these elements in order to assist policymakers in reducing the digital divide and achieving digital inclusion (Siddiquee & Islam, 2020).

Completing this initiative of the government, the country's central bank began actively utilizing technology to spread financial services to the entrances of citizens, even those in remote places. The success of BB in using digital financial technologies to help the underserved during the past decade or two warrants reevaluation, particularly in light of the pandemic-induced global economic recession and following recovery. Bangladesh unquestionably merits the title of "early adopter" in terms of digital financial advancements (Rahman, 2022a). LightCastle Partners (2020) reveals the following:

a. Interoperable Digital Payment Platform (IDPP): In January 2020, Bangladesh Bank employed a Memorandum of Understanding (MoU) with the ICT division to develop a system is implemented of digital payments within the state, where users may access all digital services through a single API (Application Processing Interface). This would facilitate transactions between various payment service players, including consumers, merchants, payment and collections, payment systems, e-wallets, banks and financial institutions, and payment scheme operators. This is now undergoing testing by Bangladesh Bank and will shortly be made available to all clients.

b. Disbursing Cash Aids using Mobile Financial Services: Using Bkash, the country's biggest MFS worker, the government distributed BDT 2,500 to 50 million needy households. The receivers were not required to pay cash-out costs, and NID confirmation was utilized to guarantee that the correct individuals received the funds. This strategy drew additional users to the environment and established extensive belief in the system, hence enhancing the reputation of MFS among all present and potential participants.

c. Pro–Internet Banking Policies: In recent times, Bangladesh Bank increased the daily limit for interbank internet transactions, including a fivefold growth for institutional customers. This policy modification would enable more consumers to conduct safe online dealings from their homes, eventually expanding the reach of online banking across the nation.

d. Micro Merchant Support: Bangladesh bank has banks, MFS, and payment services for micro-merchants to create retail accounts. This procedure does not need any additional fees, including value-added tax or tax documentation numbers. This measure has permitted connectivity at the lowest point of commerce in Bangladesh and is considered the first step toward financial intermediation at the lowest level of merchants.

3.5 Efforts of Bangladesh Bank for Mobile Banking

Global technology offers numerous advantages to the growth of small and medium-sized businesses. This perspective extends to financial manufacturing, as fintech firms remain to enter the marketplace with groundbreaking, consumer financial services, and/or products (Gazel & Schwienbacher, 2021). After graduating from low-income status, a number of significant economies have remained locked in the middle-income position for as long as twenty or thirty years. To overcome the obstacle, several qualitative modifications are required. If better education, improved health care, planned urbanization, and enhanced peace and order are not guaranteed, reaching a higher socioeconomic level alone will not be sufficient. These are crucial for achieving a sustainable economy with a better income. The extent to which we can eradicate corruption and promote good governance will also be crucial. Without progress in these areas, it is possible that we will be trapped in the "middle-income trap." Without economic diversity, development might stall. Diversification of exports is one of the most important problems. An economy depending on a single export item is susceptible to both internal and external shocks. Additionally, we must diversify our financial industry and goods. Beyond banks and nonbank financial institutions, we must build our capital market as an alternative source of growth funding. Our tax-to-GDP ratio is the lowest in all of South Asia; thus, we must also strengthen our efforts to raise income. In the fiscal year 2019–2020, the tax-to-GDP ratio was just 9.5 percent, and it is projected to reach 10 percent in the fiscal year 2023–2024. This is considerably below the minimum standard. After LDC graduation, domestic resource mobilization will play a crucial role in funding our economic operations (Khatun, 2022).

The expanding fintech business has significant effects on the financial sector, namely, in the areas of payment services, crowdfunding, capital markets, wealth management, lending, and assurance. The introduction of new products, business models, channels, and service delivery innovations has altered the financial services sector. The effect of fintech disruptions has been magnified by increased customer knowledge and expectations, digitization, favorable directive, and cost-cutting pressures (Zarrouk et al., 2021). Bangladesh's mobile business has expanded significantly over the past decade to develop the fifth-largest smartphone market in Asia-Pacific, with eighty-five million unique customers in 2017 – half of the population. By promoting digital editions and supporting the provision of important services, mobile manufacturing makes a vital involvement in Bangladesh's economy and plays an important part in achieving the government's Digital Bangladesh and Vision 2021 creativities, as well as the United Nations' SDGs. Despite having more than 90 percent of the population covered by 3G networks, Bangladesh faces a significant digital divide due to its predominantly 2G mobile market. In 2017, only one in five Bangladeshis had access to mobile internet facilities. Bangladesh exhibits one of the world's lowest internet penetration rates. Network coverage remainders a barrier to access, especially in rural and isolated portions of the country, although coverage alone does not ensure access. Despite the improvements made over the past several years, Bangladesh ranks poorly in terms of the key enablers necessary for mobile internet access to grow. In comparison to its regional rivals, the country scores below average on infrastructure and affordable enablers. Timing is also a factor in Bangladesh's gradual transition to mobile broadband technologies: the 4G/LTE spectrum auction did not take place until February 2018, subsequent similar delays to the 3G auction, making Bangladesh one of the last nations in South Asia to grant licenses for the machinery (GSMA, 2018).

In Bangladesh, mobile financial services have expanded in the last decade (Parvez et al., 2015). During the continuing COVID-19 epidemic, a constant stream of new MFS users has boosted the quantity and value of transactions and financial transfers. Rocket, a mobile banking service provided by Dutch-Bangla Bank Limited, was launched on March 31, 2011. BRAC Bank Limited launched the bKash mobile financial services app on July 21, 2011. The Bangladesh Post Office introduced Nagad, a digital banking service, on November 11, 2018, and it went live on March 26, 2019. There were 15 banks in Bangladesh that offered MFS as of April 2021, and there were more than 1 million agents, 96 million registered clients, and 36 million active accounts overall. Over 10 million transactions take place on a daily basis, totaling more than 21 billion Bangladesh taka (BDT). Between March 2020 and January 2021, a period of 11 months, there were 18 million more MFS customers (Ahmed et al., 2022). Within a period of five years, the mobile banking industry saw compound annual growth of almost 20 percent in regard to the average number of daily transactions (from December 2015 to December 2020). Due to health concerns about handling cash physically during the COVID-19 epidemic, many people began utilizing MFS to reduce health hazards (Tasreen, 2021).

When the COVID-19 pandemic broke out in March 2020, there were widespread lockdowns and an increase in the number of individuals utilizing MFS to buy necessities. As a result, the epidemic drove Bangladesh's digital payments ecosystem to unprecedented heights. Immediately after the pandemic broke out, there was a drop in economic activity due to public panic and business closures, but this was quickly followed by a steady increase in transactions. Given that access to MFS has been simpler over time, the rise in MFS payments was the most obvious. Despite the fact that the outbreak caused a decline in commerce nationwide, the surge in digital payments shows that an increasing number of individuals are switching to digital payment systems for their everyday and commercial activities. Through contactless payments, the shift to digital payment systems improved COVID-19 hygiene standards and promoted financial inclusion. Additionally, the practicality, simplicity, and expansion of digital payment methods have considerably helped crucial services like food delivery and online shopping (Ahmed et al., 2022). Rahman has compiled a list of the main steps done to digitize financial services in Bangladesh during the past ten years (2022):

a. Implementation of an automated Credit Information Bureau (CIB) in Bangladesh to promote better credit risk control and business ventures.
b. Automated check dispensation, BEFTN, the National Payment Switch, and RTGS are implemented to improve the speed and dependability of financial services.

c. Linking the Know Your Customer procedure with the National Election Commission's national database (through utilizing the NIDs).

d. The implementation of ISS (Integrated Supervision System), a connected and paperless management system, has been a tremendous success.

e. Significant modifications to the customary reporting of trade services, including the introduction of online reporting of all incoming and outgoing remittance transactions by approved dealers.

f. Bangladesh's access to finance has been transformed by the digitization of financial services (online banking, agent banking, and mobile financial services).

g. Banks in Bangladesh have already begun embracing blockchain technology, which will importantly aid the country in trade-related transactions by error-free, making them paperless, real-time, inexpensive, and quick.

Above all, importantly, thanks to Bangladesh Bank's creative initiatives, banks now use core banking software and have significantly automatic the majority of their internal and external processes. As anticipated, this push for digitalization has had a considerable beneficial influence on financial inclusion in Bangladesh. This is evident in the Financial Access Survey (FAS) done periodically by the International Monetary Fund (IMF) (Rahman, 2022a).

3.6 Conclusion

The global growth of telecommunications technology has altered the way people live and do business. In recent years, m-business (mobile business), e-business, e-commerce, and have expanded fast. Due to the worldwide growth and cost discount of mobile and internet technologies, mobile enterprises are gaining in popularity and demand at a rapid rate (Lee et al., 2012). Even though it is an emerging country, Bangladesh is a shining example of successful mobile banking and a critical driver of the transaction revolution, considering its reputation consequently. Traditional banks only served particular segments of the population, whereas mobile banking serves all components and subsections of the people, which would be a revolution for all of us (Hasan, 2020). The number of people using digital financial systems is expanding. People are becoming accustomed to living in a digital world. However, most Bangladeshi clients are unaware of MFSs. They are unaware of the potential of contemporary technology and do not make an effort to gain greater control of the situation and realize the rewards of MFS. Because Bangladesh's financial services scheme is still in its infancy, it's vital to examine the prospects and challenges of this program's impact and execution. Young people from lower- and middle-income circumstances use mobile banking at an increased rate than the rest of the country. Nevertheless, the rewards of mobile banking services are universal. Using mobile financial services transactions is more comfortable, saves time, and is less expensive than conventional banking. It is possible to acquire services via mobile phone, removing the need to physically visit bank locations and fulfill other prerequisites. Some business and government institutions use mobile financial services to pay salaries, and invoices, and conduct other banking transactions (Kumar, 2022). MFS in Bangladesh, such as Upay, bKash, Rocket, Nagad, and others, have all responded to the challenge, with help from the Bangladesh banks and government, to provide safe and secure financial services inside the nation (Gomes, 2020). Customer impressions of MFS reduced physical access, and lower cost barriers enable a far bigger quantity of the public to use uncomplicated formal sector deposits and expense services, hence assisting many small business proprietors in receiving payments and expanding their operations (Chowdhury et al., 2019). In recent years, the same survey noted a trend among businesspersons to establish their enterprises using a number of websites. E-commerce websites and Facebook boost mobile banking payments. MFS providers are therefore attempting to make their systems more user-friendly (Ahmed et al., 2022).

Bangladesh is already seeing a rapid growth in mobile financial services. If operators' interoperability and conformance are guaranteed, agency costs are minimized, and a level playing field is created, the industry will reach new heights. From funds transfer to paying for utility, education, transit, medical, and retail expenditures, the business has evolved into a one-stop shop for all kinds of activities. Financial inclusion has been accelerated due to this invention (Rahman, 2021). Although COVID-19 has flaws, one positive effect of such a dreadful situation could be a growing awareness about MFS in Bangladesh, with preference shifting to a more cashless economy due to increasing technology understanding and hygiene concerns. The epidemic will almost certainly have long-term effects, forcing people to reconsider their behavior in all areas of life and ushering in a series of changes, many of which are visible. Despite the instability, Bangladesh's MFS providers' numerous progressive activities serve as hopeful motivators for the industry's flourishing future (Gomes, 2020). The availability of metaled roads and electricity has practically transformed the culture and economy of rural Bangladesh. Numerous urban establishments, such as coffee shops, community centers, beauty parlors, workshops for expanding rural transportation and agricultural equipment, and mobile accessory stores, are transforming the rural environment into a mini-urban area. Without a doubt, over 60 percent of rural income currently comes from non-farming activity. The rapid influx of money from metropolitan regions and foreign nations into rural areas, facilitated by enhanced banking and digital financial services, has made rural Bangladesh an appealing center of commercial development. The provision of electricity in rural areas has not only alleviated the tedium of rural living, but is also boosting the growth of micro, small, and medium-sized businesses in which many women are both owners and employees. As an important component of rural change, microfinance institutions have also made substantial contributions to empowerment. Digital connectivity has been especially beneficial for spreading technology and urban lifestyles to rural places (Rahman, 2022b).

Numerous men and women are propelled into a new life cycle by a variety of personal, communal, national, and global events (Garcia & Gruat, 2003). Although digital technologies such as mobile banking might considerably increase people's access to financial services in impoverished nations like Bangladesh, they did not receive adequate attention prior to the COVID-19 epidemic. Using secondary data, this study examined the situation of mobile banking services in Bangladesh in connection to accelerating people's financial access during the COVID-19 epidemic. In spite of the fact that mobile banking began in 2011 in the United States, its acceptability by customers is growing in the wake of the recent COVID-19 outbreak as a means of acquiring financial access quickly, conveniently, and securely. People are now more anxious about hygiene than in the past. To halt the spread of the COVID-19 epidemic, individuals are compelled to create mobile banking accounts on their own mobile devices. Consequently, the number of recorded mobile banking users amplified dramatically throughout the epidemic. Different mobile banking transactions, including cash-in, cash-out, and person-to-person (P2P) transactions, have expanded dramatically during the COVID-19 epidemic as a result of shifting consumer preferences and government activities. The significance of mobile banking has also increased for mobile recharging, remittance transactions, contribution delivery, and distribution of safety net monies, among other applications (Khatun et al., 2021). The government should establish an easy platform for financial access in order to develop a digital Bangladesh and cashless society in order to combat the present pandemic. Even after the COVID-19 outbreak, measures must be taken to expand the use of electronic payment systems for social security benefits and government worker compensation. It is anticipated that these initiatives will contribute to the continued growth of mobile financial services in Bangladesh during and after the prevalence of COVID-19, thereby enhancing people's financial inclusion in the future.

4 Mobile Banking in Access to Public Services and Key Influencing Factors

4.1 Introduction

Advancements in digitization and the emergence of a competitive knowledge economy will have an important impact on the next decades of the twenty-first century. This worldwide setting necessitates that all nations maximize the potential of their youth, particularly those aiming to sustain high levels of growth and reach development on par with the club of affluent nations. Bangladesh is presently witnessing a demographic dividend that is anticipated to reach its zenith during the next two decades. To sustain the substantial economic growth of recent years, Bangladesh will need to devise credible measures to capitalize on this demographic resource. Consequently, policymakers and development practitioners are extremely interested in the youth's behaviors, worldviews, talents, and skills (Rahman, 2020). Digital technology is an unstoppable force of our time that is reshaping civilizations worldwide. Digital technology offers limitless opportunities for enhancing human well-being, but it also poses a threat to those who cannot utilize it. It relies on its deployment and utilization. In Bangladesh, like in the remainder of the emergent world, digital technology has mostly touched the population through mobile phones and mobile internet, enabling digitalized services, enterprises, and the interchange of information. Whether or whether the citizens of our nation can utilize these digital technologies to their benefit relies on their access to gadgets (e.g., mobile) and connectivity (e.g., the Internet) and, more crucially, their ability to use the available digital technologies. Citizens may be incapable to access many critical services and reap the benefits of digitalization without proper access and expertise. In addition, the digital divide, which is characterized by unequal access to technology and digital skills, is expected to result in unequal access to and inefficiency with the vast array of accessible digital services. Therefore, digitalization may not only generate new kinds of exclusion but also exacerbate existing disparities (Rabbani et al., 2020).

Individuals assimilate and absorb MFS technology. Even though the MFS market in Bangladesh is expanding, it faces obstacles such as a dearth of interoperability and price rules. Bangladesh Bank must build interoperability between MFS providers and commercial banks and implement relevant norms and supervision for the MFS business to attain its pinnacle in terms of financial addition and reasonable economic growth (Ahmed et al., 2022). During the COVID-19 epidemic, monetary manufacturing in Bangladesh has been an important challenge; nonetheless, the necessity to address the needs of consumers of financial services increases the usage of mobile banking in both rural and urban areas. The study examines the effect of customer gratification and customer devotion on rural Bangladesh's mobile banking service during the pandemic. Because the service industry is one of the most significant contributors to economic and social growth on a global scale (Yalley & Agyapong, 2017). The economic development of a nation is dependent on its financial system (Ayadi et al., 2015). Furthermore, researchers are challenged with the issue of company operations in a self-motivated and inexpensive environment. E-banking allowed a variety of client service options, such as internet banking, ATM service, and mobile banking. Technological products and services, including loans and developments, deposit management, bill systems, and e-payment, may be provided to consumers at the lowest possible cost via the electronic channel (Samadi & Skandari, 2011). The banking industry's strategy of using mobile phones to provide financial products and increase the value of customers' financial transactions over mobile networks was a necessity of the times (Taghavi-Fard & Torabi, 2011). Mobile banking is an essential concept that generates new economic streams in the expanding worldwide economy. Service quality is the most significant precondition for enduring in an inexpensive environment and contributing the finest obtainable services in order to get a sustained competitive benefit (Bala et al., 2021).

Due to the development of mobile technologies and strategies, banking customers can now admittance their accounts from any location. Many banks throughout the world have recently enabled smartphone access to financial data. Understanding what factors influence consumers' intent to utilize mobile banking is an important area of research. The goal of this study is to investigate and validate the drivers of consumers' propensity to utilize mobile banking (Ahmed et al., 2012). According to several academics, the markets for mobile payment services are in evolution, with a past of multiple attempted and failed solutions and a future of intriguing, but unpredictable, prospects involving potential new technological advancements. At this stage of development, the researchers examine the present situation of the mobile payment services market via the lens of a literature study. They examine existing literature on mobile payments, assess the numerous aspects that influence mobile payment services marketplaces, and propose future study objectives in this still-emerging topic. Modern research best covers the consumer viewpoint on mobile payments as well as technological security and trust. Unexplored subjects include the effects of cultural and socioeconomic characteristics on mobile payments and the comparability between mobile and conventional payment services (Dahlberg et al., 2008).

4.2 Data Analysis and Discussion

Demographic Facts:

This section of the Element focuses on the demographic features of the respondents who use mobile banking. Figure 2 shows the gender distribution of mobile banking users in Bangladesh, with 58 percent being males and 42 percent being females out of a total of 300 respondents.

The age distribution of the mobile banking users in Figure 3 indicates that around 80 percent fall within the 21- to 30-year age range. Around 16 percent fall within the 31- to 40-year age range, while only 4 percent of respondents are aged 40 years or above.

Figure 4 portrays the occupation classification of mobile banking users. It suggests that among 300 respondents, 55 percent of the respondents are students while 20 percent engaged in business-related activities. Additionally, 15 percent

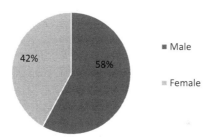

Figure 2 Gender.

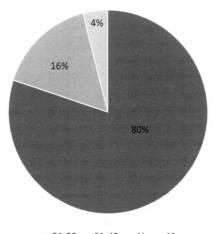

Figure 3 Age.

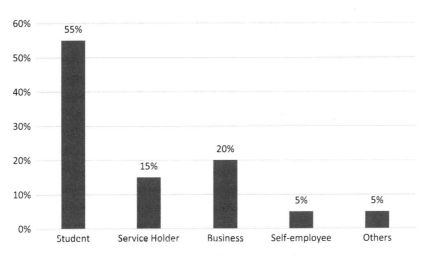

Figure 4 Classification of occupation.

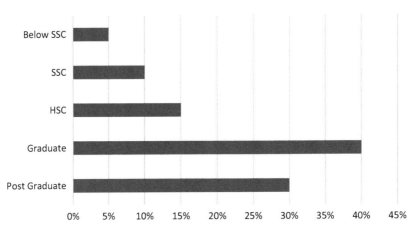

Figure 5 Educational background.

of the respondents are service holders, while 5 percent are self-employed. The remaining 5 percent belong to various other occupations.

Figure 5 provides insight into the educational backgrounds of the mobile banking users. It shows that among 300 respondents, 40 percent of the population holds graduate degrees. Another 30 percent have completed some form of postsecondary education. Furthermore, 15 percent of the users possess a Higher Secondary Certificate, while 10 percent hold a Secondary School Certificate (SSC). The remaining 5 percent have an education level lower than SSC.

Key Influencing Factors:

Figure 6 depicts the level of perceived usefulness of mobile banking. Out of 300 respondents, 65 percent agreed that mobile banking is useful. They mentioned that opening a mobile banking account allows for easy money exchange with other account holders, and transactions can be made 24/7, providing convenient public service across the country. Additionally, 11 percent strongly agreed that mobile banking eliminates the need to visit the bank multiple times, saving time and allowing for transactions from anywhere. However, 15 percent disagreed, citing issues with poor network connectivity and challenges for illiterate individuals. They expressed concerns about increased expenses due to the use of mobile banking. Furthermore, 9 percent of respondents had a neutral stance on the perceived usefulness of mobile banking.

Mobile banking also offers time-saving benefits compared to traditional banking methods. With a smartphone and internet access, users can conveniently conduct banking transactions from virtually anywhere. Therefore, the convenience of mobile banking is enhanced when users have access to a wide range of mobile devices.

Figure 7 illustrates the perceived ease of use of mobile banking in the current scenario. Among 300 respondents, 57 percent agree with the ease of use of mobile banking for public services. They mentioned that they can conveniently perform tasks such as recharge, bill payment, online payment, and money transfer through the mobile banking app at any time without needing to visit the bank. They can also directly apply for other banking services, such as home loans, personal loans, RD, and fixed deposits, from the comfort of their home using mobile banking, whether they have a smartphone or a regular phone.

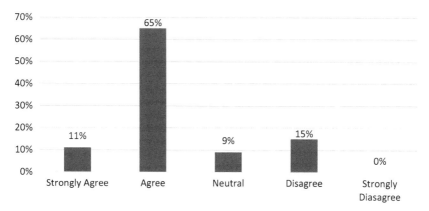

Figure 6 Usefulness of mobile banking (Source: Field Survey, 2022).

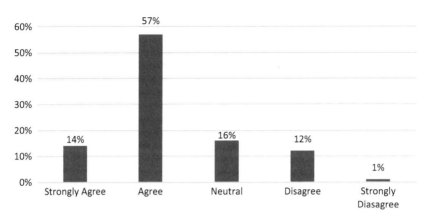

Figure 7 Perceived ease of use of mobile banking (Source: Field Survey, 2022).

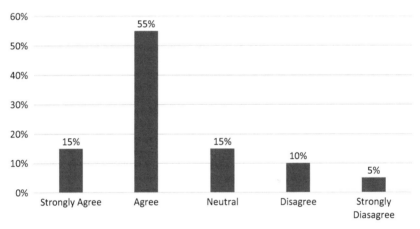

Figure 8 Trust in mobile banking (Source: Field Survey, 2022).

Additionally, 14 percent strongly agree that mobile banking usage is very easy as it allows them to avail services while staying at home with their smartphones.

On the other hand, 16 percent expressed neutrality, as they believed that some banks may charge fees while others may not for certain services. They view mobile banking as a bank that provides services to the people. Meanwhile, 12 percent disagreed with the ease of use of mobile banking, citing high service charges and the requirement of a smartphone as barriers. They perceive mobile banking as smartphone-dependent banking.

Figure 8 depicts the level of trust in mobile banking. Based on the findings, out of 300 respondents, 55 percent believe that mobile banking is trustworthy for availing public services and is useful. They view it as a secure and reliable option that provides protection against suspicious purchases. They also believe that mobile banking is as trustworthy as traditional banking systems, as it requires user authentication through user ID, password, transaction code, and so on, and safeguards against unauthorized access. They believe that mobile banking accounts and money are fully secure when availing public services.

However, 15 percent have mixed opinions, with some strongly agreeing and others remaining neutral about the trustworthiness of mobile banking for public services. On the other hand, 10 percent disagree with trusting mobile banking, expressing concerns about potential security risks, such as the possibility of hackers withdrawing money with knowledge of user ID and password, or falling victim to fake messages that result in unauthorized access to their accounts. Furthermore, 5 percent strongly disagree, citing previous experiences of hacking incidents involving money and password of banking accounts, and expressing doubts about the security and reliability of online banking systems.

Figure 9 displays the level of self-efficacy in using mobile banking for public services. The results show that out of 300 respondents, 65 percent agree, stating that they have sufficient knowledge and understanding of mobile banking and how to use it. They possess the skills, abilities, and knowledge to use mobile banking effectively, including transferring money and making transactions. Mobile banking has made bill payments more convenient and accessible, even for illiterate individuals, and has been utilized smoothly by them to increase public service.

However, 10 percent did not express their opinion on mobile banking self-efficacy. Meanwhile, 20 percent strongly agree with their self-efficacy in using mobile banking, indicating a high level of confidence. Only 5 percent disagree with their self-efficacy, mentioning a lack of knowledge about mobile banking and how to use it, especially among illiterate individuals who occasionally use

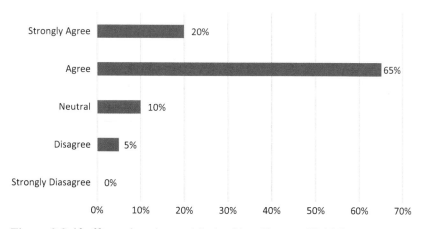

Figure 9 Self-efficacy in using mobile banking (Source: Field Survey, 2022).

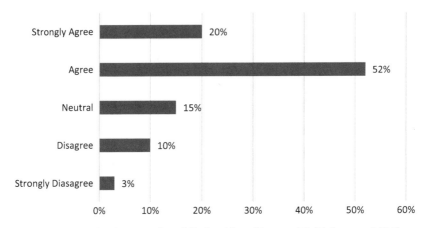

Figure 10 Attitude toward mobile banking (Source: Field Survey, 2022).

mobile banking for their children and family members. Mobile banking has played a significant role in promoting economic development through online banking.

Figure 10 displays the level of attitude toward mobile banking. Out of 300 respondents, 52 percent agreed with a positive attitude toward mobile banking. They are using various forms of electronic transactions such as e-commerce, e-banking, and e-government, and have a favorable view of mobile banking. They find the current mobile banking system easy to use and frequently use it for transactions and money exchanges due to its convenience and low cost.

Additionally, 20 percent strongly agree with the positive use of mobile banking, citing factors such as family and relatives sending money through mobile banking. On the other hand, 15 percent have neutral agreement whereas 10 percent and 3 percent have disagreement and strongly disagreement respectively with the positive use of mobile banking due to lack trust, high transaction cost, and poor network connectivity.

Figure 11 shows the level of behavioral intention toward mobile banking. In this regard, out of 300 respondents, 55 percent mentioned "Agree." They found mobile banking more flexible than manual systems and expressed the importance of SMS gateway workers providing quality service to banks and financial institutions in terms of SMS services. They expressed their willingness to use mobile banking. Additionally, 15 percent selected "Strongly Agree," while another 15 percent mentioned "Neutral." 10 percent selected "Disagree" and another 5 percent mentioned "Strongly Disagree." They expressed concerns about encountering technical and service outages, as well as high mobile banking service charges. They suggested that the bank authority should reduce costs and provide more opportunities to increase user engagement.

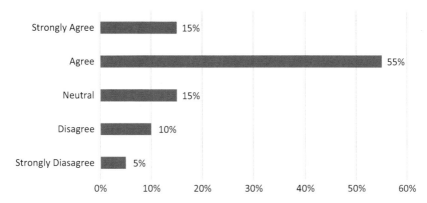

Figure 11 Behavioral intention toward mobile banking (Source: Field Survey, 2022).

4.3 Findings of the Study

a. **Perceived Usefulness:** The majority of respondents believe that mobile banking facilitates access to public services, and they utilize it without difficulty. Respondents also believed that the online mobile banking system is beneficial and effective for both rural and urban users. The concept of perceived usefulness is crucial, as it suggests that using technology would increase the quality of one's work. However, some individuals do not use mobile banking due to a lack of digital literacy and awareness. They believe that mobile banking technology would reduce fees and time requirements. On the other hand, some mobile banking services do not provide users with sufficient service.

b. **Ease of Use of Mobile Banking:** The users of mobile banking state that the system is straightforward to operate. The majority of customers use public transportation and pay their bills through mobile banking. Additionally, they can obtain low-interest loans using mobile banking. Mobile banking is easy to use, as long as someone has a smartphone or regular phone. Paying various bills through these apps provides many benefits and rebates, and anyone can purchase train and airplane tickets. If someone requires any type of bank statement, they can easily locate it here.

c. **Trust in Mobile Banking:** Most people trust the mobile banking system and have utilized its services. They have confidence in the system due to its transparency, timely work, and goodwill. However, a few people do not trust mobile banking because they have faced issues such as ID or password hacks, disappearing money, and lack of security for their accounts. Despite this, the number of mobile banking users is increasing, and people are increasingly relying on the system.

d. **Self-Efficacy of Mobile Banking:** Self-efficacy describes a person's technological understanding (Seo & Bernsen, 2016). It is defined as the belief that one can effectively carry out a specific action (Bandura, 1997). Most of the respondents have knowledge, ability, and ideas about mobile banking, but some respondents lack knowledge or ability due to a lack of digital literacy. In the future, as the digital literacy rate increases, more people will be able to use mobile banking.

e. **Attitude toward Mobile Banking:** The majority of individuals have a positive attitude toward mobile banking. They appreciate the convenience of being able to transact anytime and take advantage of other opportunities such as e-banking, e-service, e-government, and e-commerce through mobile banking. However, some individuals have a negative attitude toward mobile banking due to high costs and a lack of knowledge about how to use it. Additionally, some people have a neutral attitude toward mobile banking.

f. **Behavioral Intention toward Mobile Banking:** Around 60 percent of the total respondents have a positive behavioral intention toward mobile banking, as users find it convenient and easy to use. Mobile banking services are becoming increasingly popular in Bangladesh, with people opening accounts using their mobile numbers to facilitate fast and efficient money transfer and exchange. However, some users' behavioral intentions are negative due to concerns about issues like identity and password theft, and loss of funds.

4.4 Conclusion

Globally, mobile banking is expanding at a rapid rate. In doing so, it generates substantial doubt over the proper regulatory reaction to this newly developing service. A researcher provides a framework for seeing the design of mobile banking guidelines. Due to its location at the intersection of financial services and telecommunications, mobile banking also poses a struggle for policy and interoperability concerns, which are examined in his article. By separating payment services into their constituent pieces, mobile banking gives vital insights into the design of financial guidelines in both developed and developing nations (Klein & Mayer, 2011).

The Sustainable Development Goals (SDGs) were accepted by all UN Member States in 2015 and have since been a crucial indication of Bangladesh's progress. To achieve these objectives, Bangladesh has been utilizing its existing resources, as well as financial sources, focusing on advanced and inspired growth, and restructuring the financial system to serve all people, particularly the poor (Institute for Inclusive Finance and Development) (InM), 2021). Permitting "access to financial services for everyone" implies that individuals from all economic classes have the resources to defend themselves from unanticipated income fluctuations, save for the future, preserve a consistent cash flow, and have an overall understanding of their financial worth. It is considered that financial access allows for a higher level of life and is a mission toward reaching the SDGs (Sakina, 2022). During the COVID-19 pandemic, an extraordinary increase in the usage of fintech and e-commerce produced a paradigm change in digitalized acquisitions by customers and the use of online selling stages and digital payments by businesses. After the outbreak of COVID-19, digital payments became a safety-required means for conducting financial transactions, hence significantly expanding the role of fintech. In addition to enabling commerce, digital payments aided the government during the COVID-19 epidemic in distributing stimulus funds to businesses and individuals (Hossain & Chowdhury, 2022). How and to what degree micro, small, and medium-sized enterprises (MSMEs) have understood the assistance of fintech is relevant to their recovery from the epidemic, given the beneficial impact of fintech and digital finance in the epidemic. During this tough period of economic stagnation induced by the pandemic, the section of industrial units worst impacted has been MSMEs; therefore, their recoveries have a significant impact on their particular economies (Leach et al., 2020).

In the near future, the tradition of mobile phones to conduct financial transactions is likely to rise significantly. The widespread adoption of mobile financial services will be determined not just by technical progress but also by the level of confidence that consumers have in these new options. Mobile financial services can be segmented into mobile banking and smartphone payments; hence, legal inevitability must be recognized regarding the regulatory framework that pertains to the various activities combining banking and nonbanks. If the description of banking activity includes all applicable mobile banking activities, then prudential control of mobile banking activities falls under the competence of the competent financial market regulator. Furthermore, regulatory considerations play a role in the advancement of mobile banking in terms of the requirement to increase client confidence in the supplied services. Information security and customer protection present significant challenges. Moreover, the subcontracting of certain critical functions to mobile operators merits further consideration, since mobile operators might get intimately involved in mobile banking under certain conditions (Weber & Darbellay, 2010).

5 Summary, Recommendations, and Concluding Facts

5.1 Introduction

In the twenty-first century, digital skills have become increasingly attractive and crucial in various aspects of human life, including earning, learning, and navigating a world that is becoming more and more digital. The disparity in digital skills between different groups, such as the wealthy and the poor, men and women, and rural and urban populations, has emerged as a global problem, exacerbating existing socioeconomic inequalities. Bangladesh, like the rest of the world, is rapidly embracing digital products and services (Rabbani et al., 2020). The first-level digital divide refers to differences in individuals' access to internet connectivity, while the second-level digital divide pertains to disparities in individuals' online abilities and internet usage (Katz & Rice, 2002; Newhagen & Bucy, 2005). Traditional channels are being replaced by new technological advancements, with mobile devices emerging as the latest trend in electronic service delivery. To gain a deeper understanding of customer perspectives in the realm of electronic banking, qualitative in-depth interviews were conducted with experienced electronic banking users. The research aimed to uncover insights into customer-perceived quality, value generation based on mobile service attributes, and customer-perceived drawbacks associated with mobile phones in the context of electronic banking. The findings offer valuable information for consultants seeking to enhance their services and marketing strategies, as well as for academics identifying promising areas for future research (Ahmed et al., 2012).

In recent years, the economic sector in Bangladesh has experienced a significant growth in terms of volume and complexity. Despite notable progress in areas such as capital base, return on equity, and income, the financial sector in Bangladesh still faces challenges in providing basic financial services to large segments of the low-income population, including those engaged in rural and urban agricultural and nonfarm economic activities. However, with the emergence of opportunities for innovation, Bangladesh Bank has taken the lead in modernizing the country's payment platform and financial sector IT infrastructure. This has paved the way for more efficient and affordable mobile phone-based off-branch commercial banking services, specifically targeting underserved demographic groups. To foster a competitive and regulated environment that can effectively expand the reach of financial services, Bangladesh Bank (BB) has introduced regulatory guidelines for MFS platforms in Bangladesh (Bangladesh Bank, 2015). Digital inclusion is contingent upon internet access as a fundamental requirement. However, the discourse on the digital divide has evolved in recent years to encompass the importance of online literacy, also known as the second-level digital gap, which is necessary for effectively and efficiently utilizing the Internet. Therefore, the term "digital divide" now encompasses both disparities in internet access and disparities in online abilities, recognizing that the presence of both access and skills brings benefits, while their absence poses drawbacks (Siddiquee & Islam, 2020).

5.2 Summary of Findings

These following findings provide an overview of the key aspects related to mobile banking based on the responses received.

a. **Perceived Usefulness:** Users of mobile banking find it easy to perform transactions. Respondents expressed their belief that internet banking is a useful and effective system for both rural and urban users. It is presumed that utilizing appropriate technology would enhance the perceived utility of mobile banking users.

b. **Ease of Use of Mobile Banking:** The majority of consumers find mobile banking convenient and effortless. They use it to pay various bills and conduct product sales. Even in need of funds, they can access low-interest loans through mobile banking.

c. **Trust in Mobile Banking:** The majority of consumers have faith in the financial system when it comes to mobile banking services due to its transparency, reliability, and helpfulness. Their trust is based on a lack of major issues or problems encountered in the past.

d. **Self-Efficacy in Using Mobile Banking:** Most respondents have knowledge, skills, and an understanding of mobile banking. However, some individuals lack knowledge or skills due to a lack of education. It is crucial for everyone to have sufficient knowledge about mobile banking to utilize it effectively.

e. **Attitude toward Mobile Banking:** Users appreciate the convenience of conducting transactions anytime through mobile banking. They actively engage in mobile banking, utilizing it for e-banking, e-services, e-government, and e-commerce.

f. **Behavioral Intention toward Mobile Banking:** Mobile banking services are gaining popularity in Bangladesh. People are opening mobile banking accounts using their mobile numbers due to the ease and speed of money transfer and exchange.

5.3 Recommendations

Article 16 of the Constitution serves as a source of inspiration for the ruling party's policy commitment, as reflected in this section of its election manifesto, with a focus on the planned transformation of rural Bangladesh. The manifesto outlines a comprehensive vision that includes extensive electricity coverage, the growth of cottage industries and other businesses, improvements in healthcare and education infrastructure, and agricultural modernization. The ultimate goal is to bridge the rural–urban gap and ensure equitable living conditions for both urban and rural residents. Furthermore, the manifesto highlights the intention to address energy challenges through the development of additional biogas facilities and supports rural entrepreneurs in establishing workshops for rural transportation and agricultural machinery. Adequate funding will be allocated to support these entrepreneurial initiatives (Rahman, 2022b). While the following recommendations are not exhaustive and are limited to those resulting from this study (Parvez et al., 2015), various stakeholders within the ecosystem can implement a range of measures to overcome the remaining obstacles.

Reforms in the public administration system are necessary to ensure the provision of quality public services. Promotion and rewards should be based solely on performance and integrity, with public servants working for the current administration. They should transcend political disputes and fulfill their duties without bias. The professional integrity of public workers should not be compromised by favoritism becoming a primary career criterion. It is not only the business sector but also the general population that seeks improved government services, whether it be social safety net assistance or healthcare. Many individuals, particularly the most vulnerable and impoverished, lack the resources for self-development and, therefore, require increased government support. Enhancing the effectiveness of public services will be a crucial factor in the country's next significant leap forward. Overall, Bangladesh must strive to improve the quality of its development in the subsequent phases, transitioning from mere growth to inclusive development that encompasses both quantitative and qualitative improvements in all aspects of life (Khatun, 2022).

These following specific suggestions aim to address various aspects of mobile banking in order to enhance its usefulness, convenience, trustworthiness, self-efficacy, user attitude, and behavioral intention in the context of Bangladesh.

a. **Usefulness:** Mobile banking authorities in Bangladesh should prioritize reducing costs and service rates to make mobile banking more cost-effective and accessible for users in the local context. Moreover, they should ensure that every account includes a reliable double security feature to enhance user trust and the security of their financial transactions, which is crucial given the local cybersecurity concerns. Additionally, introducing cashback opportunities and loyalty programs can significantly enhance the usefulness of mobile banking, offering users financial incentives and rewards for their continued engagement with the service, which is particularly attractive to the cost-conscious Bangladeshi population.

b. **Convenience:** Mobile banking provides the convenience of online banking, enabling users in Bangladesh to transfer money at any time and from anywhere. To make it even more convenient in the local context, mobile banking authorities should consider optimizing their user interfaces, streamlining the user experience, and offering intuitive features for tasks like fund transfers, bill payments, and account management, which is essential to cater to users with varying digital literacy levels. It is an affordable and convenient method for sending money, saving, and obtaining loans, aligning with the financial needs of the Bangladeshi population.

c. **Trust:** To build a higher level of trust among users in Bangladesh, mobile banking authorities should prioritize user security by implementing PIN code authentication for transactions, which is vital due to the need for robust security measures in the local context. Furthermore, they should consistently provide reliable services, secure user accounts, and PIN codes, including frequent security updates, and offer digital literacy programs to educate users on maintaining their account's safety. It is also essential to ensure comprehensive protection of personal information, adhering to stringent data privacy and security regulations relevant to Bangladesh. Establishing clear and transparent communication channels with users can foster trust, ensuring that they are well informed about the security measures in place and any potential risks, which is especially important in a security-conscious environment.

d. **Self-Efficacy:** Enhancing self-efficacy among users in Bangladesh is essential. Mobile banking authorities should conduct training sessions not only to educate individuals on how to use mobile banking but to empower them with the necessary knowledge, skills, and ideas. In addition to training, providing user-friendly guides, video tutorials, and readily accessible customer support can further boost self-efficacy. Ensuring that users have easy access to resources that help them troubleshoot issues or seek assistance when needed can significantly increase their confidence in using mobile banking services effectively, considering the varying levels of digital literacy in Bangladesh.

e. **Attitude:** To improve user attitudes in Bangladesh, mobile banking authorities should focus on enhancing the user experience by providing efficient and hassle-free services. Additionally, offering incentives, such as cashback rewards, and reducing fees for money exchanges can positively influence user attitudes, particularly among price-sensitive consumers. Proactive user education campaigns, clear communication of the benefits of mobile banking tailored to the local context, and responsive customer support can further promote a positive attitude among users. Ensuring a user-friendly interface, available in local languages, and addressing user concerns promptly can go a long way in changing negative perceptions into positive ones.

f. **Behavioral Intention:** Users in Bangladesh may hesitate to use mobile banking due to slow internet speeds in certain areas. To build stronger behavioral intention among users, mobile banking authorities should prioritize improving the mobile banking experience in regions with slow internet speeds, such as remote coastal and hilly areas. This could involve collaborating with internet service providers to enhance connectivity, which is particularly relevant in areas with limited network infrastructure. Additionally, ensuring the availability of technological resources, such as easy-to-use mobile apps and responsive websites, can encourage users to engage with mobile banking services more frequently, especially in areas with varying levels of digital access. Moreover, providing reliable customer support and addressing user concerns promptly can boost users' confidence in the service, thus strengthening their intention to use mobile banking. Clear communication of the benefits of mobile banking, such as convenience and cost savings, should be tailored to the local context to encourage users to embrace this technology.

5.4 Concluding Facts

The development of mobile banking in Bangladesh faces various challenges, including infrastructure limitations, institutional barriers, and regulatory constraints. These obstacles include the absence of a nationwide backbone network, a low level of ICT adoption within the banking industry, a shortage of skilled labor and training resources, and the lack of supportive strategies, rules, guidelines, and regulations related to e-transactions. However, despite these limitations, Bangladesh Bank and the government's commitment to building a "Digital Bangladesh" have stimulated competition among scheduled banks, driving improvements in banking services and the wider implementation of e-banking. This note provides a comprehensive overview of the growth of m-banking in Bangladesh and presents future predictions to enhance readers' understanding of this subject. It covers the concept of m-banking, the current status of scheduled banks' adoption of m-banking services, and the potential scenarios for m-banking in Bangladesh. These predictions take into account the country's ongoing efforts to develop its ICT infrastructure and the level of ICT saturation in the banking sector. By considering these factors, the aim is to maximize the benefits of m-banking for both Bangladesh and the scheduled banks (Ahmed et al., 2012).

Bangladesh has undergone a significant transformation in financial access through the digitization of financial services. This transformation is crucial in ensuring an inclusive and desirable economic revival for the nation. However, it is important to acknowledge that learning through practical experience is the only viable approach. Simultaneously, careful attention must be paid to the sustainability and affordability of digital infrastructure and internet access. Furthermore, the establishment of a policy framework that prioritizes consumer benefits is essential. This framework should encompass aspects such as ensuring interoperability and creating a favorable tax structure. Additionally, it is crucial to gain and maintain the trust of clients. Digital financial service providers must ensure that consumers adapt to the "new normal" and that fraudsters do not undermine the carefully crafted ecosystem. By focusing on these aspects, Bangladesh can harness the full potential of digitization in the financial sector and drive its economic growth effectively (Rahman, 2022b).

To provide exceptional customer-centric service, it is crucial to develop and maintain momentum by demonstrating actions and achievements. While the overall high consumer satisfaction indicates that we are on the right track, further investigation is necessary to understand the variations between different components and services. This study has a few limitations that should be addressed. Firstly, it only considers five independent criteria, overlooking potential variables that may impact consumer happiness. Demographic factors such as gender, age, and race, which could influence mobile banking adoption and satisfaction, were not examined. Additionally, geography and other demographic factors can also influence consumer expectations and satisfaction, warranting extensive examination. A future study could explore how cultural and socioeconomic factors affect the relationship between service quality and customer happiness. Furthermore, the sample size used in this study is relatively small compared to the population size. As the number of mobile banking users continues to rise, conducting longer research is necessary to identify consumer behavior trends and enhance the quality of mobile banking services (Jahan & Shahria, 2021). In order to bridge the rural–urban divide that persists in our development journey, it is imperative to implement planned strategies for the sustainable transformation of rural Bangladesh through the provision of essential services. The commitments outlined in the constitution and the aspirations of the Sustainable Development Goals (SDGs) highlight the need for a systematic approach to developing infrastructure and other services, gradually transforming villages into sustainable and livable compact cities. Increased coordination and collaboration between national and local administrations are indispensable for planning and implementing this sustainable transformation of villages. Furthermore, the involvement of the commercial sector, nongovernmental organizations, and civil society organizations is essential in driving this transformative effort (Rahman, 2022b).

Abbreviations

API	-	Application Processing Interface
APIs	-	Application Programming Interfaces
ATM	-	Automated Teller Machine
BB	-	Bangladesh Bank
BDT	-	Bangladesh Taka
BTRC	-	Bangladesh Telecommunication Regulatory Commission
CFA	-	Confirmatory Factor Analysis
CIB	-	Credit Information Bureau
CRM	-	Customer Relationship Management
DBBL	-	Dutch Bangla Bank Limited
GDP	-	Gross Domestic Product
GoB	-	Government of Bangladesh
ICT	-	Information Communication and Technology
ID	-	Identity Documents
IDPP	-	Interoperable Digital Payment Platform
IMF	-	International Monetary Fund
ISS	-	Integrated Supervision System
LDC	-	Least Development Country
LGIs	-	Local Government Institutions
MFSs	-	Mobile Financial Services
MoU	-	Memorandum of Understanding
NCR	-	National Capital Region
NID	-	National Identification Card
NPS	-	Net Promoter Score
PDA	-	Personal Digital Assistant
PIN	-	Personal Identification Number
SDG	-	Sustainable Development Goal
SIM	-	Subscriber Identity Module
SMS	-	Short Message Service
SMEs	-	Small and Medium-sized Enterprises
TAM	-	Technological Acceptance Framework
UDC	-	Union Digital Centers
UN	-	United Nations
USD	-	United States Dollar
UTAUT	-	Unified Theory on Acceptance and use of Technology
WAP	-	Wireless Application Protocol

References

Achieng, B. M., & Ingari, B. K. (2015). Factors Influencing the Adoption of Mobile Banking in Kenya's Commercial Banks: A Case of Kenya Commercial Bank (KCB) Kilindini Branch. *International Journal of Scientific and Research Publications*, 5(10), 1–14.

Ahmed, A., Uddin, S. R., & Hassan, S. R. (2022). Early Career Researchers: Factors Affecting Consumer Behaviour in Mobile Financial Services in Bangladesh. *Asia-Pacific Sustainable Development Journal*, 29(1), 142–167.

Ahmed, S. S., Rayhan, S. J., Islam, M. A., & Mahjabin, S. (2012). Problems and Prospects of Mobile Banking in Bangladesh. *Journal of Information Engineering and Applications*, 1(6), 16–34.

Akhter, N., & Khalily, B. (2017). Impact of Mobile Financial Services on Financial Inclusion in Bangladesh. *Institute for Inclusive Finance and Development (InM), Working Paper*, 52. Tokyo: Asian Development Bank Institute.

Akhter, N., & Khalily, M. B. (2020). An Analysis of Mobile Financial Services and Financial Inclusion in Bangladesh. *Indian Journal of Human Development*, 14(2), 213–233.

Alam, M. P., & Sarowar, G. (2020). Financial Inclusion: A Tool to Fight Poverty in BD. CUFBDA. https://cufbda.org/financial-inclusion/.

Al-Debei, M. M., Al-Lozi, E., & Papazafeiropoulou, A. (2013). Why People Keep Coming Back to Facebook: Explaining and Predicting Continuance Participation from an Extended Theory of Planned Behaviour Perspective. *Decision Support Systems*, 55(1), 43–54.

Ajzen, I. (1991). The Theory of Planned Behavior. *Organisational Behavior and Human Decision Processes*, 50(2), 179–211.

Anayasi, F. I., & Otubu P. A. (2009). Mobile Phone Technology in Banking System: Its Economic Effect. *Research Journal of Information Technology*, 1(1), 1–5.

Andrew, W. (2009). Mobile Banking in Developing Countries: A Case Study on Kenya, Vaasan Ammattikorkeakoulu University of Applied Sciences. www.theseus.fi/bitstream/handle/10024/4402/Wambari_Andrew.pdf? sequen [accessed on 10 May 2022].

Ashta, A. (2017). Evolution of Mobile Banking Regulations: A Case Study on Legislator's Behavior. *Strategic Change*, 26: 3–20.

Ayadi, A. (2005). Value Creation in Mobile Banking. *Development and Comp Systems*, 1–6. University Library of Munich, Germany. https:// EconPapers.repec.org/RePEc:wpa:wuwpdc:0508010.

Ayadi, R., Arbak, E., Naceur, S. B., & De Groen, W. P. (2015). Financial Development, Bank Efficiency and Economic Growth across the Mediterranean. In R. Ayadi, M. Da-browski, & L. De Wulf (Eds.), *Economic and Social Development of the Southern and Eastern Mediterranean Countries* (pp. 219–233). Switzerland: Springer.

Bala, T., Jahan, I., Al Amin, M., et al. (2021). Service Quality and Customer Satisfaction of Mobile Banking during COVID-19 Lockdown; Evidence from Rural Area of Bangladesh. *Open Journal of Business and Management*, 9(5), 2329–2357.

Balakrishnan, L., & Sudha, V. (2016). Factors Affecting Mobile Banking Services–An Empirical Study. *ISBR MANAGEMENT JOURNAL ISSN (Online)-2456–9062*, 1(2), 1–18.

Bandura, A. (1997). *Self-efficacy: The Exercise of Control*. New York: Freeman.

Barnes, S. J., & Corbitt, B. (2003). Mobile Banking: Concept and Potential. *International Journal of Mobile Communications*, 1(3), 273–288.

Batten, A., Doung, P., Enkhbold, E., et al. (2015). The Financial Systems of Financially Less Developed Asian Economies: Key Features and Reform Priorities. *Asian Development Bank Economics Working Paper Series* (450). Tokyo: Asian Development Bank.

Bangladesh Bank (2015). Regulatory Guidelines for Mobile Financial Services (MFS) in Bangladesh. www.bb.org.bd/aboutus/draftguinotification/guide line/mfs_final_v9.pdf [accessed on 12 June 2022].

Bangladesh Bank & University of Dhaka (2017). *An Impact Study on Mobile Financial Services (MFSs) in Bangladesh*. Dhaka: Bangladesh Bank and University of Dhaka.

Banna, H., Hassan, M. K. & Rashid, M., (2021). Fintech-Based Financial Inclusion and Bank Risk-Taking: Evidence from OIC Countries. *Journal of International Financial Markets, Institutions and Money*, 75, 1–20

Barua, D., & Akber, S. M. (2021). Customers' assessment on E-Banking Service Quality in Bangladesh: Challenges and Strategies. *American Finance & Banking Review*, 6(1), 14–25.

Bampo, M., Ewing, M. T., Mather, D. R., Stewart, D., & Wallace, M. (2008). The Effects of the Social Structure of Digital Networks on Viral Marketing Performance. *Information Systems Research*, 19(3), 273–290.

Baten, M. A., & Kamil, A. A. (2010). E-Banking of Economical Prospects in Bangladesh. *Journal of Internet Banking and Commerce*, 15(2), 1–10.

Bangladesh Bank (BB) (2012). Mobile Financial Services in Bangladesh: An Overview of Market Development (Bangladesh Bank Policy Paper, pp. 1–28). Bangladesh Bank.

Bangladesh Bank (BB) (2019). *Survey on Impact Analysis of Access to Finance in Bangladesh*. Dhaka: Bangladesh Bank (BB).

Barnes, S. J., & Corbitt, B. (2003). Mobile Banking: Concept and Potential. *International Journal of Mobile Communications*, 1(3), 273–288.

Bhattacherjee, A., & Sanford, C. (2006). Influence Processes for Information Technology Acceptance: An Elaboration Likelihood Model. *MIS Quarterly*, 30(4), 805–825.

Blank, G., & Groselj, D. (2014). Dimensions of Internet Use: Amount, Variety, and Types. *Information, Communication & Society*, 17(4), 417–435.

Brixiova, Z., Li, W., & Yousef, T. (2009). Skill Shortages and Labor Market Outcomes in Central Europe. *Economic Systems*, 33(1), 45–59.

BRAC Institute of Governance & Development (BIGD) (2020). Transforming Customer Experiences in Public Services (Mobile Banking, Agent Banking, and SSN Allowance Payment): What Have We Learned?, 1(3), https://bigd.bracu.ac .bd/wp-content/uploads/2020/05/Transforming-Customer-Experiences-in-Public-Services_Policy-Brief-2.pdf [accessed on 15 June 2022].

Boston Consulting Group (BCG) (2011). The Socio-Economic Impact of Mobile Financial Services: Analysis of Pakistan, Bangladesh, India, Serbia and Malaysia. www.telenor.com/wp-content/uploads/2012/03/The-Socio-Economic-Impact-of-Mobile-Financial-Services-BCG-Telenor-Group-2011.pdf.

Bisschoff, C., & Clapton, H. (2014). Measuring Customer Service in a Private Hospital. *Problems and Perspectives in Management*, 12(4), 43–54.

Billon, M., Marco, R., & Lera-Lopez, F. (2009). Disparities in ICT Adoption: A Multidimensional Approach to Study the Cross-Country Digital Divide. *Telecommunications Policy*, 33(10–11), 596–610.

Carter, L., & Weerakkody, V. (2008). E-Government Adoption: A Cultural Comparison. *Information Systems Frontiers*, 10(4), 473–482.

Carr, D. (2007). The Global Digital Divide. *Contexts*, 6(3), 1–58.

Canuto, O. (2013). Mobilising Development via Mobile Phones. Growth and Crisis. http://blogs.worldbank.org/growth/mobilizing-development-mobile-phones [accessed on 2 December 201].

Chowdhury, A. Y., Hossain, A. K. M. A., Habib, M. M., & Yue, X. G. (2019). Role of Mobile Financial Service in Promoting Online Small Business in

Bangladesh. *IETI Transactions on Social Sciences and Humanities*, 5, 140–148.

Chitungo, S. K., & Munongo, S. (2013). Extending the Technology Acceptance Model to Mobile Banking Adoption in Rural Zimbabwe. *Journal of Business Administration and Education*, 3(1), 51–79.

Chen, L. D. (2008). A Model of Consumer Acceptance of Mobile Payment, *International Journal of Mobile Communications*, 6(1), 32–52.

Dalim, S. H. (2020, April 8). Silent Role of MFS to Keep the Economy Going. The Daily Star, www.thedailystar.net/opinion/economics/news/silent-role-mfs-keep-the-economy-going-1890613.

Davis, F. D. (1989). Perceived Usefulness, Perceived Ease of Use, and User Acceptance of Information Technology. *MIS Quarterly*, 13(3), 319–340.

Daniel, E. (1999). Provision of Electronic Banking in the UK and the Republic of Ireland. *International Journal of Bank Marketing*, 17(2), 25–34.

Dahlberg, T., Mallat, N., Ondrus, J., & Zmijewska, A. (2008). Past, Present and Future of Mobile Payments Research: A Literature Review. *Electronic Commerce Research and Applications*, 7(2), 165–181.

DFID (2018) DFID Digital Strategy 2018 to 2020: Doing Development in a Digital World. www.gov.uk/government/publications/dfid-digital-strat egy-2018-to-2020-doing-development-in-a-digital-world/dfid-digital-strat egy-2018-to-2020-doing-development-in-a-digital-world.

Dona, P. D., Mouri, S. I., Hasan, M., & Abedin, M. Z. (2014). Significance of Exponential Uses of Mobile Financial Services (MFS) in Bangladesh. *Global Journal of Management and Business Research*, 14(4), 93–102.

Dixit, N., & Datta, S. K. (2010a). Acceptance of E-Banking among Adult Customers: An Empirical Investigation in India. *Journal of Internet Banking and Commerce*, 15(2), 1–11.

Dixit, N., & Datta, S. K. (2010b). Customers Perception on Internet Banking and Their Impact on Customer Satisfaction and Loyalty: A Study in Indian Context. *Journal of Computing*, 2(7), 131–135.

Donner, J. & Tellez, C. A. (2008). Mobile Banking and Economic Development: Linking Adoption, Impact, and Use. *Asian Journal of Communication*, 18(4), 318–332.

European Commission (EC) (2010). Public Services in the European Union & in the 27 Member States: Statistics, Organisation and Regulations. www.ceep.eu/images/stories/pdf/Mapping/CEEP_mapping%20experts% 20report.pdf.

Ehsan, Z. A., Musleh, N., Gomes, V., Ahmed, W., & Ferdous, M. D. (2019). The Usage of Mobile Financial Services in Bangladesh. MPRA Paper No. 109974. https://mpra.ub.uni-muenchen.de/109974/1/MPRA_paper_109974.pdf.

Fuchs, C. (2017). Information Technology and Sustainability in the Information Society. *International Journal of Communication*, 11, 2431–2461.

Gazel, M., & Schwienbacher, A. (2021). Entrepreneurial Fintech Clusters. *Small Business Economics*, 57(2), 883–903.

Gallivan, M. J., Spitler, V. K., & Koufaris, M. (2005). Does Information Technology Training Really Matter? A Social Information Processing Analysis of Coworkers' Influence on IT Usage in the Workplace. *Journal of Management Information Systems*, 22(1), 153–192.

Gefen, D., Karahanna, E., & Straub, D. W. (2003). Trust and TAM in Online Shopping: An Integrated Model. *MIS Quarterly*, 527(1), 1–90.

Georgi, F. & Pinkl, J. (2005): Mobile Banking in Deutschland – Der zweite Anlauf. *Die Bank*, (3), 57–61.

Greenacre, J., & Buckley, R. P. (2014). Using Trusts to Protect Mobile Money Customers. *Singapore Journal of Legal Studies*, 59–78.

Grove, S. J., Carlson, L., & Dorsch, M. J. (2007). Comparing the Application of Integrated Marketing Communication (IMC) in Magazine ads across Product Type and Time. *Journal of Advertising*, 36(1), 37–54.

Garcia, A. B., & Gruat, J. V. (2003). A Life Cycle Continuum Investment for Social Justice, Poverty Reduction and Sustainable Development. *Ginebra: ILO*, 1–64.

Gomes, V. (2020, May 8). Mobile Financial Services Soaring in a Pandemic-Stricken Bangladesh. The Daily Star, www.thedailystar.net/toggle/news/ mobile-financial-services-soaring-pandemic-stricken-bangladesh-1900507.

Government of Bangladesh (GoB) (2010). Digital Bangladesh for Good Governance. https://erd.portal.gov.bd/sites/default/files/files/erd.portal.gov.bd/ page/60daef34_a889_4a94_a902_f3a4a106762b/BDF2010_Session%20VI% 20(1).pdf.

GSMA (2018). Country Overview: Bangladesh: Mobile Industry Driving Growth and Enabling Digital Inclusion. https://data.gsmaintelligence.com/ api-web/v2/research-file-download?id=30933394&file=Country%20over view%20Bangladesh.pdf [accessed on 19 June 2022].

Hasan, M. T. (2020). M-Banking: The Transaction Revolution in Bangladesh. *Science Research*, 8(4), 98–107.

Hasan, M. (2021, January 17). Mobile money in the COVID-19 Pandemic. The Daily Star, www.thedailystar.net/supplements/mobile-financial-services/ news/mobile-money-the-covid-19-pandemic-2028889.

Hernandez, K. (2019). Barriers to Digital Services: Adoption in Bangladesh. K4D Helpdesk Report 573. Brighton: Institute of Development Studies. https://assets.publishing.service.gov.uk/media/5d7f5d0ced915d52428dc0ce/

573_Leave_No_One_Behind_in_a_Digital_World_Barriers_and_Constraints_in_Bangladesh.pdf.

Hernandez, K., & Roberts, T. (2018). Leaving No One Behind in a Digital World: An Extended Literature Review. https://assets.publishing.service.gov.uk/media/5c178371ed915d0b8a31a404/Emerging_Issues_LNOBDW_final.pdf.

Himel, M. T. A., Ashraf, S., Bappy, T. A., et al. (2021). Users' Attitude and Intention to Use Mobile Financial Services in Bangladesh: An Empirical Study. *South Asian Journal of Marketing*, 2(1), 72–96.

Hilbert, M. (2010). When Is Cheap, Cheap Enough to Bridge the Digital Divide? Modeling Income Related Structural Challenges of Technology Diffusion in Latin America. *World Development*, 38(5), 756–770.

Hossain, M., & Chowdhury, T. T. (2022). COVID-19, Fintech, and the Recovery of Micro, Small, and Medium-Sized Enterprises: Evidence from Bangladesh. *ADBI Working Paper* 1305. Tokyo: Asian Development Bank Institute. www.adb.org/publications/covid-19-fintech-and-the-recovery-of-micro-small-and-medium-sized-enterprises-evidence-from-bangladesh [accessed on 15 June 2022].

Hossain, R. (2021, September 13). Digital Banking for Bangladesh. *Daily Sun*, www.daily-sun.com/printversion/details/576244/Digital-banking-for-Bangladesh [accessed on 18 September 2022].

Hossain, M. A., & Haque, M. Z. (2014). Prospects and Challenges of Mobile Banking in Bangladesh. *Journal of Business*, 35(2), 165–186.

Hossain, M., Hossain, M. J., Samsuzzaman, M., & Islam, M. T. (2017). Mobile Payment System and Its Development in Bangladesh. Proceedings of Melbourne International Business and Social Science Research Conference 2017, Rendezvous Hotel, Melbourne, 28–30. www.aabl.com.au/aablConference/public/documents/pdf/2018_03_15_12_10_24_248.pdf.

Huda, F., & Chowdhury, T.A. (2017). Prospect of E-Banking in Bangladesh: New Way to Make Banking Electronic. *Asian Economic and Financial Review*, 7(9), 509–518.

Islam, M. L. (2022, April 8). Open Banking: The New Customer Experience. Daily Sun, www.daily-sun.com/post/614667/Open-Banking:-The-New-Customer-Experience [accessed on 15 July 2022].

Islam, M. S. (2013). Mobile Banking: An Emerging Issue in Bangladesh. *ASA University Review*, 7(1), 123–130.

Islam, M. Z. (2018, August 20). Mobile Data Leads to Internet Boom. The Daily Star, www.thedailystar.net/news/business/telecom/mobile-data-service-leads-to-internet-boom-in-bangladesh-1623310 [accessed on 16 August 2022].

Islam, N., Mustafi, M., Rahman, M., et al. (2019). Factors Affecting Customers' Experience in Mobile Banking of Bangladesh. *Global Journal of*

Management and Business Research: A Administration and Management, 19(5), 37–49.

Islam, M. S., Karia, N., Soliman, M. S. M., et al. (2017). Adoption of Mobile Banking in Bangladesh: A Conceptual Framework. *Review of Social Sciences*, 2(8), 1–8.

Islam, N., Rahman, M. N., Nower, N., et al. (2019). Factors Affecting Customers' Experience in Mobile Banking of Bangladesh. *Global Journal of Management and Business Research*, 19(5), 1–18.

Islam, M. M., Rashid, H., & Alam, M. G. R. (2015). Secure Electronic Payment: Proposed Method for the Growth of E-Commerce in Bangladesh. *Asian Business Review*, 5(2), 89–96.

Ivatuary, G. & Mas, I. (2010). The Early Experience with Branchless Banking. Focus note no.46. www.ssrnpapers.com [Accessed on 25 October 2015].

Jahan, N., & Shahria, G. (2021). Factors Effecting Customer Satisfaction of Mobile Banking in Bangladesh: A study on Young Users' Perspective. *South Asian Journal of Marketing*, 3(10), 60–76.

Kabir, M. R. (2013). Factors Influencing the Usage of Mobile Banking: Incident from a Developing Country. *World Review of Business Research*, 3(3), 96–114.

Kabir, M. H., Sadrul Huda, S. S. M., & Faruq, O. (2020). Mobile Financial Services in the Context of Bangladesh. *Copernican Journal of Finance & Accounting*, 9(3), 83–98.

Katz, J. E., & Rice, R. E. (2002). *Social Consequences of Internet Use: Access, Involvement, and Interaction*. Cambridge: MIT Press.

Kahandawa, K., & Wijayanayake, J. (2014). Impact of Mobile Banking Services on Customer Satisfaction: A Study on Sri Lankan State Commercial Bank. *International Journal of Computer and Information Technology*, 3(3), 546–552.

Koivu, T. (2002). Do Efficient Banking Sectors Accelerate Economic Growth in Transition Countries. SSRN 1015710.

Kumar, D. (2022). Prospects and Challenges of Mobile Financial Services (MFS) in Bangladesh. In P.C. Lai (Ed.) *Handbook of Research on Social Impacts of E-Payment and Blockchain Technology* (pp. 320–341). Hershey, PA: IGI Global.

Khatun, M. N., Mitra, S., & Sarker, M. N. I. (2021). Mobile Banking during COVID-19 Pandemic in Bangladesh: A Novel Mechanism to Change and Accelerate People's Financial Access. *Green Finance*, 3(3), 253–267.

Khraim, H. S., Al Shoubaki, Y. E., & Khraim, A. S. (2011). Factors Affecting Jordanian Consumers' Adoption of Mobile Banking Services. *International Journal of Business and Social Science*, 2(20), 96–105.

Khan, M. R., & Chaipoopirutana, S. (2020). Factors Influencing Users' Behavioral Intention to Reuse Mobile Financial Services in Bangladesh. Journal of Management and Marketing Review, 5(3), 155–169.

Khatun, F. (2022, January 20). Public Sector Needs to Keep Pace with Private Sector. The Business Standard, www.tbsnews.net/supplement/public-sector-needs-keep-pace-private-sector-359749 [accessed on 16 August 2022].

Klein, M. U., & Mayer, C. (2011). Mobile Banking and Financial Inclusion: The Regulatory Lessons. *World Bank Policy Research Working Paper* (5664). Washington, DC: World Bank

Laforet, S., & Li, X. (2005). Consumers Attitude Towards Online and Mobile Banking in China. *International Journal of Bank Marketing*, 23(5), 362–380.

Liza, F. Y. (2014). Factors Influencing the Adoption of Mobile Banking: Perspective Bangladesh. *Global Disclosure of Economics and Business*, 3(2), 199–220.

LightCastle Partners (2020, December 31). Digital Payments in Bangladesh: A Road to Growth and Stability. *LightCastle Analytics Wing*, www.light castlebd.com/insights/2020/12/digital-payments-in-bangladesh-a-road-to-growth-and-stability/ [accessed on 14 May 2022].

Leach, M., MacGregor, H., Scoones, I., & Wilkinson, A. (2020). Post-Pandemic Transformations: How and Why COVID-19 Requires Us to Rethink Development. *World Development*, 138, 1–11.

Lee, Y. K., Park, J. H., Chung, N., & Blakeney, A. (2012). A Unified Perspective on the Factors Influencing Usage Intention Toward Mobile Financial Services. *Journal of Business Research*, 65(11), 1590–1599.

Luarn, P., & Lin, H. H. (2005). Toward an Understanding of the Behavioral Intention to Use Mobile Banking. *Computers in Human Behavior*, 21(6), 873–891.

Madden, M., & Fox, S. (2006). Riding the Waves of "Web 2.0." *Pew Internet and American Life Project*, 5, 1–7.

Mahajan, N. (2015). E-Governance: Its Role, Importance and Challenges. *International Journal of Current Innovation Research*, 1(10), 237–243.

Martin, B. (2004). What Is Public about Public Services? Washington, DC: World Bank. www.publicworld.org/files/WhatIsPublic.pdf.

Mattila, M. (2003). Factors Affecting the Adoption of Mobile Banking Services. *Journal of Internet Banking and Commerce*, 8, 8–12.

Montoya, M. M., Massey, A. P., & Khatri, V. (2010). Connecting IT Services Operations to Services Marketing Practices. *Journal of Management Information Systems*, 26(4), 65–85.

Modak, T. (2022, August 19). Mobile Banking Transactions Hit Second-Highest in June. The Business Standard, www.tbsnews.net/economy/

mobile-banking-transactions-hit-second-highest-june-480242 [accessed on 18 September 2022].

Nabi, M. G., Sarder, M. M. R., Moula, M. G., & Sarder, M. W. (2017). Do Mobile Financial Services Promote Ethical Banking in Bangladesh. *Bangladesh Economic Association*, 2017, 1–17.

Nasri, W. (2011). Factors Influencing the Adoption of Internet Banking in Tunisia. *International Journal of Business and Management*, 6(8), 143–160.

Newhagen, J. E. & Bucy, E. P. (2005). *Routes to Media Access: Living In The Information Age*. Belmont: Wadsworth.

Ono, H., & Zavodny, M. (2007). Digital Inequality: A Five Country Comparison Using Microdata. *Social Science Research*, 36(3), 1135–1155.

Parvez, J., Islam, A., & Woodard, J. (2015). Mobile Financial Services in Bangladesh: A Survey of Current Services, Regulations, and Usage in Select USAID Projects. Dhaka, Bangladesh: USAID.

Parvin, A. (2013). Mobile Banking Operation in Bangladesh: Prediction of Future. *The Journal of Internet Banking and Commerce*, 18(1), 1–15.

Payne, A.F., Storbacka, K., and Frow, P. (2008). Managing the Co-creation of Value. *Journal of the Academy of Marketing Science*, 36, 83–96.

Porteous, D. (2006). *The enabling environment for mobile banking in Africa*, Report commissioned by DFID, London.

Prins, R., & Verhoef, P. C. (2007). Marketing Communication Drivers of Adoption Timing of a New E-Service among Existing Customers. *Journal of Marketing*, 71(2), 169–183.

Rabbani, M., Matin, M., Zahan, I., Islam., M. S. & Rahman, S. (2020). Digital Literacy and Access to Public Services in Bangladesh. BRAC Institute of Governance and Development, https://bigd.bracu.ac.bd/study/digital-literacy-and-access-to-public-services-in-bangladesh/ [accessed on 16 May 2022].

Rahman, A. (2022a, February 15). In Search of Digital Financial Inclusion in Bangladesh. The Daily Star, www.thedailystar.net/recovering-covid-reinventing-our-future/fourth-industrial-revolution-and-digital-transformation/news/search-digital-financial-inclusion-bangladesh [accessed on 14 May 2022].

Rahman, A. (2022b, January 23). My Village, My Town. Daily Sun,www.daily-sun.com/printversion/details/601078/'My-Village-My-Town' [accessed on 15 June 2022].

Rahman, M. F. (2021, January 17). The Future of Mobile Financial Services in Bangladesh. The Daily Star, www.thedailystar.net/supplements/mobile-financial-services/news/the-future-mobile-financial-services-bangladesh-2028885.

Rahman, S. (2020). Towards a Digitalized Bangladesh: How Prepared Are Today's Youth? BIGD Research Brief, Digitization Series 07. Dhaka: BRAC Institute of Governance & Development (BIGD).

Rahman, M. L. (2016, February 1). E-Governance and Bangladesh. The Daily Star, www.thedailystar.net/25th-anniversary-special-part-1/e-governance-and-bangladesh-210577.

Rahman, M. A., Qi, X., & Islam, M. (2016). Banking Access for the Poor: Adoption and Strategies in Rural Areas of Bangladesh. *Journal of Economic & Financial Studies*, 4(3), 1–10.

Rahman, M. F. (2015, July 15). Mobile Banking to Get a Further Boost. The Daily Star, www.thedailystar.net/business/mobile-banking-get-further-boost-112576.

Rahman, M. F. (2014, March 4). Mobile Banking Key to Financial Inclusion. The Daily Star, www.thedailystar.net/mobile-banking-key-to-financial-inclusion-14002 [accessed on 10 July 2022].

Rashid, A. T., & Elder, L. (2009). Mobile Phones and Development: An Analysis of IDRC-Supported Projects. *The Electronic Journal of Information Systems in Developing Countries*, 36(2), 1–6.

Rosa, J. A., & Malter, A. J. (2003). E-(Embodied) Knowledge and E-Commerce: How Physiological Factors Affect Online Sales of Experiential Products. *Journal of Consumer Psychology*, 13(1–2), 63–73.

Sakina, K. (2022, January 27). Importance of Demand Side Factors for Financial Services and Its Provision in Bangladesh. Research & Professional Development Center (RPDC). https://bbsrpdc.com/opinion-piece/details/importance-of-demand-side-factors-for-financial-services-and-its-provision-in-bangladesh-1/ [accessed on 19 July 2022].

Samadi, A., & Skandari, S. (2011). The Effect of Service Quality on Customer Satisfaction MELi Bank of Toysergan City (Based on SERVQUAL Model). *Journal of Management*, 21, 30–40.

Sadekin, M. S., & Shaikh, M. A. H. (2016). Effect of E-Banking on Banking Sector of Bangladesh. *International Journal of Economics, Finance and Management Sciences*, 4(3), 93–97.

Sarma, M., & Pais, J. (2011). Financial Inclusion and Development. *Journal of International Development*, 23(5), 613–628.

Seo, D., & Bernsen, M. (2016). Comparing Attitudes Toward E-Government of Non-users versus Users in a Rural and Urban Municipality. *Government Information Quarterly*, 33(2), 270–282.

Sharma, S., Ahmed, S., & Hossain, M. M. (2022). Meaning of New Means: Exploring the Economic Impact of Mobile Banking on Rural Bangladesh.

International Journal of Innovation in the Digital Economy (IJIDE), 13(1), 1–18.

Shareef, M. A., Kumar, V., Kumar, U., & Dwivedi, Y. K. (2011). E-Government Adoption Model (GAM): Differing Service Maturity Levels. *Government Information Quarterly*, 28(1), 17–35.

Shadat, M., Bin, W., Islam, M., Zahan, I., & Matin, M. (2020). Digital Literacy of Rural Households in Bangladesh. Dhaka: BRAC Institute of Governance and Development (BIGD), https://bigd.bracu.ac.bd/wp-content/uploads/2020/10/Working-Paper_Digital-Literacy-of-Rural-Households-in-Bangladesh.pdf [accessed on 12 May 2022].

Shah, M., & Clarke, S. (Eds.). (2009). *E-banking Management: Issues, Solutions, and Strategies: Issues, Solutions, and Strategies*. Hershey, PA: IGI Global.

Sharma, S., & Hossain, M. M. (2015). The Socio-Economic Impact of Mobile Banking on Rural Bangladesh. International Conference on Economics and Finance. Kathmandu, Nepal.

Shaikh, S. A. (2013). Islamic Banking in Pakistan: A Critical Analysis. *Journal of Islamic Economics, Banking and Finance*, 9(2), 45–62.

Shrestha, S. K. (2013), Mobile Banking and Customer Satisfaction. *DAV Research Journal of Tribhuvan University*, 2, 1–6.

Singh, S. (2014). The Impact and Adoption of Mobile Banking in Delhi. *International Research Journal of Business and Management*, 1(7), 19–31.

Siddiquee, M. S. H., & Islam, M. S. (2020). *Understanding the First and Second Digital Divides in Rural Bangladesh: Internet Access, Online Skills, and Usage*. Dhaka: BRAC Institute of Governance and Development (BIGD), BRAC University.

Syvertsen, T. (1999). The Many Uses of the "Public Service" Concept. *Nordicom Review*, 20(1), 5–12.

Taghavi-Fard, M. T., & Torabi, M. (2011). The Factors Affecting the Adoption of Mobile Banking Services by Customers and Rank Them (Case Study: Bank Tejarat In Tehran, Iran). *Journal Excavations Business Management*, 3, 136–162.

Tasreen, Z. (2021, March 25). The MFS Industry is Sprightlier Today than it was Two Years Ago. And it is Thanks to Nagad. Dhaka Tribune, https://archive.dhakatribune.com/business/2021/03/26/the-mfs-industry-is-sprightlier-today-than-it-was-two-year-ago-and-it-is-thanks-to-nagad [accessed on 17 April 2022].

Tomaszewicz, A. A. (2015). The Impact of Digital Literacy on E-Government Development. *Online Journal of Applied Knowledge Management the Impact of Digital Literacy on E-Government Development*, 3(2), 45–53.

United Nations Conference on Trade and Development (UNCTAD) (2016). *Services Policy Review of Bangladesh (II)*. New York: United Nations.

Van Deursen, A. J., Van Der Zeeuw, A., De Boer, P., Jansen, G., & Van Rompay, T. (2019). Digital Inequalities in the Internet of Things: Differences in Attitudes, Material Access, Skills, and Usage. *Information, Communication & Society*, 24, 258–276.

Vota, W. (2017). Five Barriers to Mobile Financial Services in Bangladesh, ICT Works, www.ictworks.org/5-barriers-to-mobile-financial-services-in-bangla desh/#.X_3d-ugzYdV [accessed on 12 October 2021].

Waughen, K., In, S., Enterprise, F., & Walton, S. M. (2015). The Digital Divide: A Digital Bangladesh by 2021. *International Journal of Education and Human Developments*, 1(3), 1–8.

Warkentin, M., Gefen, D., Pavlou, P. A., & Rose, G. M. (2002). Encouraging Citizen Adoption of E-Government by Building Trust. *Electronic Markets*, 12(3), 157–162.

Welch, B. (1999). Electronic Banking and Treasury Security. Sawston, UK: Woodhead.

Weber, R. H., & Darbellay, A. (2010). Legal Issues in Mobile Banking. *Journal of Banking Regulation*, 11(2), 129–145.

Yalley, A. A., & Agyapong, G. K. (2017). Measuring Service Quality in Ghana: A Cross- Vergence Cultural Perspective. *Journal of Financial Services Marketing*, 22, 43–53.

Yesmin, S., Paul, T. A., & Uddin, M. M. (2019). bKash: Revolutionising Mobile Financial Services in Bangladesh?. In A. Sikdar & V. Pereira (Eds.), *Business and Management Practices in South Asia* (pp. 125–148). Singapore: Palgrave Macmillan.

Yu, C. S. (2012). Factors Affecting Individuals to Adopt Mobile Banking: Empirical Evidence from the UTAUT Model. *Journal of Electronic Commerce Research*, 13(2), 104–121.

Zarrouk, H., El Ghak, T., & Bakhouche, A. (2021). Exploring Economic and Technological Determinants of Fintech Startups' Success and Growth in the United Arab Emirates. *Journal of Open Innovation: Technology, Market, and Complexity*, 7(1), 50.

Zillien, N., & Hargittai, E. (2009). Digital Distinction: Status-Specific Types of Internet Usage. *Social Science Quarterly*, 90(2), 274–291.

Zubayer, M., Faruq, O., & Hasan, M. K. (2019). Factors Influencing the Choice of Mobile Banking Services in Bangladesh: An Exploratory Analysis. *Journal of Green Business School*, 2(1), 1–14.

Cambridge Elements $\equiv$

Economics of Emerging Markets

Bruno S. Sergi
Harvard University

Editor Bruno S. Sergi is an Instructor at Harvard University, an Associate of the Harvard University Davis Center for Russian and Eurasian Studies and Harvard Ukrainian Research Institute. He is the Academic Series Editor of the Cambridge *Elements in the Economics of Emerging Markets* (Cambridge University Press), a co-editor of the *Lab for Entrepreneurship and Development* book series, and associate editor of *The American Economist*. Concurrently, he teaches International Economics at the University of Messina, Scientific Director of the Lab for Entrepreneurship and Development (LEAD), and a co-founder and Scientific Director of the International Center for Emerging Markets Research at RUDN University in Moscow. He has published over 150 articles in professional journals and twenty-one books as author, co-author, editor, and co-editor.

About the Series

The aim of this Elements series is to deliver state-of-the-art, comprehensive coverage of the knowledge developed to date, including the dynamics and prospects of these economies, focusing on emerging markets' economics, finance, banking, technology advances, trade, demographic challenges, and their economic relations with the rest of the world, as well as the causal factors and limits of economic policy in these markets.

Cambridge Elements $\equiv$

Economics of Emerging Markets

Elements in the Series

Diagnosing Human Capital as a Binding Constraint to Growth: Tests, Symptoms and Prescriptions
Miguel Angel Santos and Farah Hani

The Economics of Digital Shopping in Central and Eastern Europe
Barbara Grabiwoda and Bogdan Mróz

Can BRICS De-dollarize the Global Financial System?
Zongyuan Zoe Liu and Mihaela Papa

Advanced Issues in the Green Economy and Sustainable Development in Emerging Market Economies
Elena G. Popkova

Banking Sector Reforms: Is China Following Japan's Footstep?
M. Kabir Hassan and Mohammad Dulal Miah

COVID-19 and Islamic Finance
M. Kabir Hassan and Aishath Muneeza

Harnessing Sovereign Wealth Funds in Emerging Economies toward Sustainable Development
Mona Mostafa El-Sholkamy and Mohammad Habibur Rahman

The Emerging Economies under the Dome of the Fourth Industrial Revolution
Mark Esposito and Amit Kapoor

On the road to economic prosperity – The role of infrastructure in Ghana
Tuan Anh Luong and Zenas Azuma

Banking Stability and Financial Conglomerates in European Emerging Countries
Pavla Klepková Vodová, Iveta Palečková and Daniel Stavárek

The Paradox of Gender Equality and Economic Outcomes in Sub-Saharan Africa: The Role of Land Rights
Evelyn F. Wamboye

Mobile Banking and Access to Public Services in Bangladesh: Influencing Issues and Factors
M. Kabir Hassan, Jannatul Ferdous and Hasanul Banna

A full series listing is available at: www.cambridge.org/EEM

Printed in the United States
by Baker & Taylor Publisher Services